/591

POLICING
SCOTLAND

POLICING
SCOTLAND

PAUL GORDON

Scottish Council for Civil Liberties

Published by
Scottish Council for Civil Liberties
146 Holland Street, Glasgow G2 4NG.

Typeset and printed by
Aberdeen People's Press Ltd. (T.U.)

ISBN 0 906502 02 0 paper
ISBN 0 906502 03 9 cloth

Trade distribution by Scottish and Northern Book Distribution
Co-operative Ltd., 45-7 Niddry Street, Edinburgh.

CONTENTS

INTRODUCTION

The police in Scotland, like too many institutions of that country, have been the subject of little serious scrutiny. What little has been written, mainly accounts of local forces or personal anecdotal memoirs, has been primarily concerned with notable incidents and personalities. This absence has had a number of effects.

Firstly, it has meant that there is widespread ignorance about the police in Scotland and few people appear to understand how the police are organised, how they are controlled and what they actually do. At a time when the police are more and more the subject of debate and scrutiny there is a need to provide some basic information about how the police developed so that we can understand the situation today and can identify differences between policing in Scotland and the rest of the country. But there is a need too to provide factual information about the police today so that debate about policing can take place in an atmosphere of knowledge and understanding of what is being talked about rather than in one of ignorance.

Secondly, the absence of scrutiny of the police in Scotland today has seriously affected our capability to defend civil liberties. It has led to a lack of awareness and knowledge of policing as it is in Scotland, as opposed to what happens elsewhere. It is almost certainly true for example that people living in Scotland will be more aware of what happens in London than of what happens in their own home towns. Attention is therefore distracted from the home situation and problems, if they are seen at all, are located elsewhere and, therefore, civil liberties must be defended elsewhere. The home situation is either seen as unproblematic and unworthy of attention and understanding or as providing a pale reflection of problems elsewhere.

In some respects this may be true. Problems of policing London may well also be problems in Dundee but often they are not and it does little good to look without success for such problems while the real issues, less dramatic perhaps and less obvious, elude us. It is unfortunate but true that radicals and the 'left' in general in Scotland have been prone to this kind of thinking, fostered in part by the London-centrism of the British left, and by the Scottish media which, with a few exceptions, has shown little inclination towards investigation or enquiry.

In this short study then I have tried to do two things. Firstly, I have attempted to sketch—no more than that— the historical development of policing in Scotland, showing not only what happened but also why it happened in the way it did. (It is worth pointing out in this respect the absence of existing historical research which serves as a context in which the development of the police may be placed and understood, especially the absence of historical writings on Scottish criminal law and the legal system). Secondly, I have tried to provide an account of policing as it is today with particular emphasis on those areas which most affect our civil liberties. Nearly all of the information on which this account is based is taken from published sources—official police reports, parliamentary papers, newspapers, journals etc. There are sure to be many gaps and omissions and the extent to which this account is incomplete or even inaccurate reflects the extent to which information is withheld from the public on matters of obvious public interest and importance.

The monitoring of the agencies and institutions of the state is, of course, a continuing task for those engaged in the protection of civil liberties and democratic rights and to this end further information on the subjects covered by this study will be gratefully received.

Paul Gordon
May 1980

ACKNOWLEDGEMENTS

In writing this book I have been fortunate in having had the generous assistance of a number of friends and colleagues who read parts of the text, forced me to clarify ideas, corrected errors, supplied information or directed me to sources. I offer my thanks to them all, particularly Douglas Allen, Chaz Ball, Deborah Haase, Hilary Idzikowska, Kenneth McNeil, Steve Peak, George Rosie, Joe Sim, Professor Christopher Smout and Bob Thomson. Alison MacMillan was a patient and efficient typist and Alan Marshall and Denise Pierrot invaluable advisers on technical matters.

The material for this study was provided primarily by the Scottish Council for Civil Liberties and by State Research but I also benefitted from the efforts of the staffs of the Mitchell Library, Glasgow and Glasgow University Library. Publication was made possible by a generous grant from the Joseph Rowntree Social Service Trust.

Especial thanks are due to Tony Bunyan and Martin Kettle, both of the State Research Group, who not only suggested the project but whose encouragement and criticism proved invaluable, and to David Godwin of SCCL who in this as in so many other projects was a close friend and invaluable adviser.

None of the above are in any way responsible for any errors of fact, opinions expressed or conclusions drawn, nor should these be taken necessarily to reflect the position of the Scottish Council for Civil Liberties.

PART ONE

HISTORICAL DEVELOPMENT

In order to understand the development of the modern system of policing it is necessary to have some understanding of the way in which law was enforced before such a system came into existence. This aspect of legal and social history is not well documented and the following account merely attempts a sketch which may provide some of the background to the formation and development of the new, full time, professional forces in the nineteenth century.

1. The Old Police

The means by which law is enforced has always been inseparable from the existing social structure. In the middle ages it was part of the feudal system and those nobles who had been granted land by the crown ('Vassals') not only had to render military service when required and maintain a castle for the purposes of defence in return but were also delegates of the crown in certain matters of authority and government and could therefore conduct their own courts, both criminal and civil. These courts were generally supervised by the king's chamberlain who travelled the country on tours of inspection.

In the twelfth century the office of sheriff was established in Scotland on the English model and the sheriff became the king's military and financial representative, responsible for maintaining the royal castle and leading the local army, and responsible too for law enforcement within the sheriffdom.

He conducted his own courts (inspected by the crown justiciar) and in time came to deal with appeals from the courts of the vassals. Along with his depute, and sheriff officers or sergeants appointed by him, he could apprehend alleged offenders and had the power forcibly to enlist public assistance in doing so by raising 'hue and cry', it being an offence to refuse.

In the fourteenth, fifteenth and sixteenth centuries, however, central control over these local royal representatives was considerably eroded due on the one hand to a series of wars with England and France and on the other to the failure of royal government: 'In the century after the death of Bruce in 1329, two Scottish kings (David II and Robert III) reigned for a total of thirty-five years with such desperate incompetence that in the words of one chronicler justice herself seemed an outlaw from the kingdom'. In addition, from the death of James I in 1437 to the early seventeenth century every Scottish monarch came to the throne as a child and between 1406 and 1587 there were nearly one hundred years of minority rule and regency (1) which fostered intense faction fighting among the nobility and led to the strengthening of local power at the expense of the central government and administration. Thus the sheriff was no longer a servant removable when he failed in his functions but the office became hereditary and the property of the most powerful local baron. The other vassals extended the jurisdiction of their courts and their powers of punishment and many obtained grants of regality giving them, in effect, all the powers of the crown within their own territories even to the extent of formally excluding royal servants (such as the chamberlain) and royal writs.

In an attempt to reassert central control, James VI had, even before the union of the Scottish and English kingdoms in 1603, tried to implement a series of reforms. Landowners and baillies were made responsible for the good behaviour of tenants and those living on their property; in 1597 all Highland landowners were ordered to produce titles to their lands and provide sureties for their good behaviour, anyone failing to do either losing his lands; special commissions were granted to deal with lawbreakers in specific areas (a joint English/Scottish Border Commission of 40 well equipped horsemen was set up to deal primarily with cattle thieving—a seventeenth century Special Patrol Group); as Ulster had been colonised by Scots so James tried less successfully also to colonise parts of the Highlands and Islands with lowlanders.(2) James also attempted to introduce into Scotland 'the laudable custom of England', the Justice of the Peace, who would not only deal promptly with offenders but who would also, it was hoped, provide a measure of supervision over the vassals and sheriffs.

In order to carry out their functions the Justices were empowered to appoint constables having powers of arrest and also, like the sheriff, being able to enlist public assistance to quell disturbances. In parishes the number of constables appointed was two while in towns and burghs the number varied with the size of the population. Generally, each served for a period of six months and their wages were paid out of fines made up where necessary by funds from central government. The constables had a number of duties. They were charged with apprehending vagrants, vagabonds, 'night walkers', and suspected persons and with searching for 'jesuits, seminarie priests, or trafficking papists' (3). They were also responsible for ensuring that every person entitled to do so maintained whatever arms and armour were appropriate to his position. Their duties were not, however, solely concerned with the suppression of crime and the maintenance of the peace but they were generally responsible for building and maintaining roads and for keeping their area clean. In this respect they appear to have been given powers of magistrates to try and fine offenders. (4).

It was this duality of function along with the political strength of the sheriffs and other nobles which prevented James' reforms having any fundamental effect. Although there was a general improvement in law enforcement during James' reign one legal historian notes that 'these ad hoc reforms however touched only the fringes of the problem. They were irregularly and imperfectly applied'. Of the Justices, he continues 'Their powers were derided by the populace. Armed bands sometimes invaded their sittings and they were subject to the constant opposition of the holders of the heritable jurisdictions…'(5).

In addition to the Constables, every town at this time maintained its own system of watchmen or Town Guard consisting of all adult male citizens (or replacements provided by them) under the command of soldiers. Smout describes the Edinburgh City Guard, popularly known as 'The Toon Rottens', as 'a body whose qualifications to keep the peace were more like those of the Chelsea pensioners than a modern police force: the guard was small, elderly, weakly armed and not very ready to withstand violence, though it could tackle a helpless drunk and frighten a pickpocket.' (6). Smout also points out that the City Guard, especially in the seventeenth century, was quite incapable and often unwilling to deal with popular disturbances or riots. It had in any case disgraced itself in the public eye when in 1736 on the orders of its commanding officer, Captain John Porteous, it had fired on a crowd at an execution killing several innocent bystanders. Porteous was convicted of murder, sentenced to death, but given a reprieve of six weeks whereupon he was taken by a crowd from the prison and hanged at the place of public execution. All of this took place without any opposition from the City Guard, the military or the magistrates and led to a heavy corporate fine being imposed on the burgh by central government for its failure to bring the leaders to justice—'Magistrates seem thereafter to have taken their duties of controlling and preventing mobs somewhat more seriously, though in the absence of an effective police force they were still sometimes reduced to timely capitulation rather than suppression'.(7) If this was the case in Scotland's capital there is little reason to believe that the Town Guard was any more effective in any other city and reports of urban riots almost invariably refer to the military, not the Town Guard, as the main public order force.

As far as the towns were concerned then, the origins of the new police forces of the nineteenth century are to be found at least partially in this dual system of JP constables and Town Guards, even though both were to co-exist with the new police for some years. In Edinburgh the City Guard existed until 1817 and the Constables until the 1860s (8).

In rural areas the origins of the police lie primarily in the system of 'rogue money' which had its origins in the 'Act for the Disarming of the Highlands' of 1724. This was one of the repressive measures taken by the government after the abortive Jacobite rising of 1715 and allowed for money to be levied for the purposes of 'apprehending, subsisting and prosecuting criminals'. Although the purpose of the levy was not formally extended to cover the maintenance of police forces until 1839 rudimentary police forces were probably set up before then. Rogue money was initially levied by freeholders, that is landowners or wealthy tenants, and after 1833 by Commissioners of Supply, central government appointees who were responsible for levying land tax in their county and who came to exercise many of the functions of County Councils. At the same time as the rogue money system was established the Black Watch regiment was formed from clans who had been loyal to the King for the specific purpose of policing the disaffected areas of the Highlands and a general process of militarisation of the Highlands got under way in the building of Telford's and Wade's famous networks of roads and bridges for speedy military transportation and the building of Fort Augustus as a supplement to Fort William. (Further repressive measures were to follow the equally abortive rebellion of 1745 in the proscription of the tartan and Highland dress until 1782; the forfeiture of estates; and the further extension of Wade's network with the building of Fort George and the settlement of loyal soldiers in the various highland towns (9). Wade's work was to prove useful to the authorities a century later when it enabled the prompt dispatch of troops to enforce evictions of tenant farmers during the clearances.

While there can never be a hard and fast distinction between the two functions of any police system—the suppression of crime on the one hand, and the maintenance of public order on the other—the Constables, Town Guards and rogue money system were, in the main, employed for the first function. The second was primarily the responsibility of various military forces. As already noted the Black Watch regiment was formed specifically for this function but there were two other sections which were used for domestic purposes: Fencible Regiments, which were raised by individuals, usually large landowners, for service within Britain, whose members were permanently on service and ready for action; and Volunteer Corps which were part time, composed of civilians who were paid for their drilling time and which were usually restricted to service in their immediate locality. (Their function was spelled out clearly by the Duke of Portland during the Militia Riots of 1797: 'The maintenance of the internal Peace of the Country and the support of the Civil Authorities was the leading principle of their institution, and the consideration which influenced Government to approve and countenance it.' (10). Both these kinds of regiment existed also in England.

Scotland however lacked any Militia such as existed in England, that is a compulsory levy of adult men, similar to but less extensive than conscription in that a ballot of all those eligible was held to see who should actually serve. From the authorities point of view the Militia was probably the best of the three types of force in that it was centrally controlled, comparatively cheap, could be mobilised quickly and was available for use anywhere in Britain. That no such force had been established in Scotland was probably due to official fear initially of Jacobitism, later of popular democratic ideas which had been adopted from the American and French revolutions. Indeed, when in response to the French Revolution and the threat of invasion a Militia Bill for Scotland was published in 1793 (it was later defeated) a correspondent wrote from Glasgow to the Lord Advocate, Henry Dundas: 'I am fully convinced that it would be highly improper to trust arms in the hands of the lower classes of people here and in Paisley... the "friends of the people" are I know very fond of the Idea which is at least a presumption against the proposal of the Measure'.(11)

By 1797, however, panic at the French Revolution had increased sufficiently for another attempt to establish a Scottish Militia, in addition to which it had become clear to the authorities that the other regiments, Fencibles and Volunteers, could not be relied on. In 1794, several mutinies had broken out in Fencible Regiments, when they were asked to do service in England and during the meal riots of the 1790s and early 1800s, Volunteers had not only refused on several occasions to take action against rioters but had fraternised with them and joined in their protest. One sheriff-substitute described them as 'rascals who have received His Majesty's pay for three years past, and took this first opportunity of refusing to do their duty and joining in the riot.'(12). The Militia Act was passed in 1797 amid considerable popular opposition (13). The organisational framework for such a force had been laid three years previously in the establishment in Scotland of a network of Lords Lieutenants who after 1802 were to play an important role in the mobilisation of the local Militia but whose main function was to be the collation of political intelligence for the use of central government. Dundas, the Lord Advocate wrote to them that their task was 'the preservation of internal tranquility against any who, either in conjunction with Foreign Enemies or activated by their own Evil Dispositions, might be inclined to disturb it.'(14)

NOTES

1. Smout, p. 33.
2. ibid. p. 99-106.
3. Adam, p. 136.
4. Adam, op cit.
5. Irvine Smith 'The Transition to the Modern Law', in Stair Society.
6. Smout, p. 344.
7. Smout, p. 210.
8. Adam, p. 146.
9. Smout, p. 208-9.
10. quoted in Logue, p. 43.
11. quoted in Logue, p. 76.
12. quoted in Logue, p. 46.
13. see Logue, Chapter 3 for a full account.
14. quoted in Logue, p. 77.

2. The New Police

At least two attempts had been made, in 1778 and 1788, to establish a police force in Glasgow before the passing of the Glasgow Police Act in 1800 which established Scotland's first statutory force. (It is interesting to note that Patrick Colquhoun who reformed the Thames River Police and was an important influence on the eventual policing of London generally, was born in Dumbarton near Glasgow and was Lord Provost of Glasgow in 1782/3 before moving to London a few years later. It is likely that he had some influence also on the formation of the Glasgow Police and the Greenock Police which was formed at the same time). It succeeded where the previous attempts had failed because it empowered the police commissioners to levy rates to maintain the force. Glasgow's example was followed by Edinburgh in 1805, Paisley (1806), Gorbals (1808), Perth (1811), Aberdeen (1818), Calton (1819), Airdrie (1822) and Dundee (1824), that is in areas which had recently undergone rapid growths in population as a result of the growth of industrial capitalism, and the concomitant migration from country to town (1). At least a dozen such forces existed before the passing of the first police act of general application in 1833 (2), which permitted but did not compel the larger and more important burghs to adopt its provisions, in particular to elect Commissioners of Police who would appoint police officers and levy rates to maintain them. Although these local forces all predate the Metropolitan Police which was established in 1829 and is commonly reckoned to be the first of the modern forces, two points have to be made.

Firstly, the early Scottish police forces were probably not substantially different from the rudimentary forces which existed in England at the same time and which form a bridge between the old and the new police. Secondly, it has to be remembered that the idea of 'police' in the nineteenth century was far wider than its present day meaning. Perhaps more so Scotland than in England it referred as much to general civic and municipal government as it did to what we understand today by policing. The acts which established police forces spoke of a 'General System of Police' which included paving, lighting, street cleaning and so on and the 'new' police were not only responsible for maintaining the peace but had a responsibility for keeping the streets clean and generally for enforcing local bye-laws regarding hygiene and sanitation. Thus in 1819 the clerk of police in Edinburgh was dismissed for overcharging the police commissioners £258 in one year alone for brooms (3).

About a dozen places took advantage of the 1833 Act to set up police forces and acts of 1847, 1850 and 1862 extended its provision to other burghs and 'populous places'. The most important of these was the General Police and Improvement Act 1850 which appears to have led to the establishment of over 30 forces and by 1860 nearly all of Scotland's urban areas had their own police. In rural areas, as already noted, the rogue money system permitted the establishment of early policing systems and rudimentary forces before it was formally permitted by the County Police Act 1839 to use the rogue money levy to maintain police forces. In 1832, for example, a police force was formed in Haddingtonshire in the east of Scotland in an attempt by the local landowners to deal with an increasingly organised working class in the area (4). The 1839 Act was a result of similar fears and followed representations to the Home Office from the Lord Lieutenant of Fife about concern in the county at organisation among the miners and religious strife between the established and other churches. The legislation closely followed the Lord Lieutenant's suggestions (5) and about 16 rural forces were to be formed in the two years after it was passed, two years which were also the peak years of the Chartist movement in Scotland. (A similar development occurred in England where the County Police Act 1839 was, according to Bunyan, 'rushed through parliament as one means of combatting Chartism.'(6).

Unlike their English counterparts who were generally re-
luctant to form police forces and had to be compelled to do so
by the County and Borough Police Act 1856, the Scottish
counties mostly did so of their own volition and less than a
dozen counties required to be compelled to do so by the provisions of the Police (Scotland) Act 1857. As Bunyan points out
in relation to England the development of the police at this
time did not simply result from an official recognition of the
value of police forces but was linked to developments in the
criminal justice system as a whole. This was true of Scotland
also where prisons were brought under central state control
in 1839 and transportation as a form of punishment was being
brought to an end in the 1850s and 60s, partly because Aus-
tralia was becoming too valuable a colony for this kind of use,
partly because of the costs involved but also because it was
seen as not being sufficiently punitive. There was therefore recognition of the fact that people who would formerly have been
transported (and who would probably have remained in Aus-
tralia) would now be imprisoned at home eventually to be
released back into society and there therefore had to be a more
efficient general system of police for the surveillance and
control of such people (7).

By the 1860s then Scotland was being policed by regular
forces which were mainly controlled and directed at a local
level. In urban areas such control was the function of the
Police Commissioners some of whom were elected by the rate-
payers, some of whom were nominated by the magistrates and
town council; in rural areas it was the function of the Commissioners of Supply and, after 1857, Police Committees composed of a number of Commissioners plus the Lord Lieutenant
of the county and the Sheriff. Control by central government
had also begun however not only in the statutory compulsion
to form forces but also more generally through the 1857 act, in
the establishment of the Inspectorate of Constabulary for Scotland who was (and is) appointed by central government. A
certificate of efficiency from the inspector was necessary
before police committees could claim the central government
grant of twenty five per cent of the cost of maintaining the
force.

The new police was therefore formed over a long period in a piecemeal and largely unsystematic way to replace agencies—the constables, the Town Guards, Militia etc—which had been adequate for the needs of a feudal social system which gave rise to them but which was clearly incapable of dealing with the problems which the eighteenth century and the breakdown of that system presented. Thus as we have seen the constables lacked any real authority in the eyes of the public; the Town Guards could not cope with popular disturbances and occasionally would not as they sympathised with those they were asked to suppress; and the loyalty of the various military forces (other than the regular army) could never be presumed. In the towns the new police had the task of policing the new urban proletariat and the new urban poor which the industrial revolution and the development of industrial capitalism had created. This meant primarily the enforcement of the criminal law and the innumerable municipal rules and bye-laws regulating the use of space which the general systems of police had introduced. In the countryside the police were preoccupied, as were their employers, with the vagrancy of the new rural dispossessed which the industrial revolution had also created and which they saw not only as bad in itself but also the cause of innumerable crimes and offences against property. Thus Alfred John List, a police officer who had been sent from London to organise the police in Haddingtonshire and whose 'Practical Treatise on the Rural Police' is one of the few documents on nineteenth century policing which survives today, identified the main duties of the rural police as 'the prevention of crime and the suppression of vagrancy' and noted that 'it is invariably found that the more pernicious crimes against property are generally committed by depredators who migrate from larger towns or adjacent counties' (8) and in his preface to the Treatise he stated that in the first week of the Haddingtonshire Police 100 vagrants had been turned out of the county and it was to the subject of vagrancy that List was to return several years later when he gave evidence to the House of Lords Select Committee on County and Police Burgh systems in Scotland in 1868. List's preoccupation with vagrancy was shared by other members of the propertied classes as is shown by the numerous testimonials which he appended to his Treatise. Thus Lady Blantyre stated that List's police system was 'of indefinite service in relieving her of the numerous beggars who used to pass through the Lennoxlove grounds.' (9).

In terms of public order, that is dealing with popular disturbances, riots, strikes, pickets and so on, the transition from the old to the new police systems was much more gradual and for most of the nineteenth century action against strikers, demonstrators, the unemployed was taken by the militia or by the regular army, although on occasion the two forces, police and military would act together as they did in 1848 in Glasgow against the large unemployed workers' demonstration, action which led to a public enquiry at the brutality involved and the eventual resignation of the chief constable. Similarly, in the Highlands during the clearances joint forces would enforce evictions and, at other times, the military would act as a back up force where the police were insufficient to the task. Prebble's account of the Highland Clearances indicates that on a number of occasions the first attempt at an eviction would be made by bailiffs or sheriff officers, the second by the police, and the third by the military (10). By 1870/80, however, the police were generally regarded as capable of dealing with such disturbances themselves although the army, then as now, remained as a force to take over when they failed.

There were a number of reasons why it was seen as necessary to transfer the public order function of the army to the police. Firstly, as already noted, the loyalty of the militia and other domestic military forces could not always be presumed; during the Highland Clearances the authorities and the landowners brought in non-Scottish soldiers because the Scots occasionally showed reluctance to evict their fellow country people. An informant had written in 1813 to Viscount Sidmouth, for example, that 'Most of the local militiamen are either themselves of the number who are dispossessed or entertain the same sentiments. A Military Force therefore of a different description has become necessary. There are however few troops in the North of Scotland' (11) and in relation to the same period Prebble notes the use of non-Scottish regular soldiers against the Highlanders; 'The presence of the 21st in the Highlands at this time of uneasiness was probably no accident of posting. There is a cumulative security to be got from using one racial minority for the suppression of another, and although the 21st was nominally a Scots regiment—(The Royal Scots Fusiliers)—the men in its ranks were mostly Irish, pressed into service by force of famine'.(12) (The same was true also during the days of the Red Clydeside in 1919 when Highland and English troops were brought into Glasgow in preference to troops from Lowland Scotland). Secondly, the army was increasingly required abroad to police the colonies, acquiring new territories and suppressing popular rebellions in others. Thirdly, it was increasingly being seen by the ruling class that while the army could deal with disturbances in the short term, in the long term its use exacerbated rather than reduced class violence. There was a need therefore for a force of a different kind and it was the new police which filled the gap and by 1856, during a miners' strike the Government Mines Inspector could say that 'the remedy for strikes is permanent mounted police' (13).

How the police came to maintain this clearly repressive function and at the same time win the confidence of the working class which they were policing was a complex process which is beyond the scope of this short history but it may be partially ascribed to the role of the police in patrolling working class areas where, despite the fact that they were regularly attacked at first, they came to be seen as offering some form of protection to individual members of the working class.

That most of the country had police forces did not mean that they were being efficiently policed and there were considerable differences in terms of wages and conditions, numbers of officers, resources etc. from one area to another. The early reports of the Inspector of Constabulary identified as the main concerns the appalling living conditions of the lower ranks in the force, the disparities in pay, which was generally low, and the absence of internal discipline. Despite all this there appears to have been no lack of recruits especially in the years of high unemployment. In 1847 during a six month period 173 men, including 86 Irish, joined the Glasgow force, although 106 were dismissed in the same period—71 for being drunk on duty, 11 for being absent without leave, 20 for being worn out and unfit for further service and 4 for assaulting prisoners (14). Training too was non-existent and there was generally no co-operation between the various forces. Colonel Kinloch, a former regular army officer who was the first Inspector of Constabulary argued consistently in his reports for legislation to abolish the smaller forces, especially since in 1859 he had certified nearly half of them as inefficient, but it was not until 1929 that the process of amalgamation really got under way.

Some police forces had begun to adapt the new scientific advances of the nineteenth century to police work and adopt a more systematic approach to investigation and detection. Glasgow claims to have had its first detective officer in 1819 who was to be exclusively involved in the investigation of crimes and who began to keep records of all crimes reported in the city and personal descriptions of all those arrested but throughout the country the investigation of crime remained for some time the practical responsibility of the procurator fiscal and only gradually was it handed over to the police. (Even today the fiscal remains ultimately responsible for the investigation of crime. See Appendix, page 124). Indeed, the Inspector of Constabulary was to note after the Second World War that it was only the war which had encouraged many forces to establish detective branches. Record keeping, when it existed at all, was therefore very rudimentary. A photographic register of people released from prison was established in Aberdeen, Inverness, Glasgow and Edinburgh in 1891 for the use of all forces in the area and similar registers established in other major towns in 1893—an extension of internal prison surveillance to the outside and to an ex-prisoner's freedom. This was the main record system until the issuing of Scottish Criminal Record Cards in 1926. Other changes which occured during this period include the introduction of the telegraph and the telephone in the 1860s and 1800s respectively and the introduction of the police box system in the 1890s. It has to be emphasised that such innovations in policing were introduced unevenly throughout the country. The major cities, especially Glasgow, Edinburgh and Aberdeen, were generally in advance of the rest of the country where changes could be extremely slow to come.

In the same period changes took place in respect of the control of the police. During the nineteenth century Scottish police matters were dealt with at central government level by the Home Secretary acting on the advice of the Lord Advocate, the senior law officer for Scotland, and it was only in 1885 that the office of Secretary of State for Scotland was established. At a local level, county councils were established in 1889 and were given some, but not all, responsibility for the police in that the powers of the Commissioners of Supply were transferred to standing Joint Committees of seven county counccillors and seven Commissioners who were retained for this purpose alone and it was only in 1929 that Commissioners of Supply were abolished altogether and the county council became the police authority for county police forces. In 1892 the Burgh Police (Scotland) Act put the final touches to policing in the towns by providing that every burgh and town had to have a police force although all but a few already had established forces.

Nationally, the police had begun to organise as workers for better pay and conditions and, as Bunyan points out, they were the first group within the public sector to form a trade union (15). The London police had gone on strike in 1872 and 1890 and the first nationwide police strike came in 1918. The Scottish police appear not to have participated despite the fact that there was considerable support and membership in Scotland of the National Union of Police and Prison Officers (NUPPO) which was affiliated to the Trades Union Congress and there had been in 1911 a rank and file campaign in Scotland for a weekly rest day for police officers. Participants in the strike were dealt with severely, and generally there was a purge of union activists throughout the country. In January 1919 a more conservative Scottish Police Union was formed as a breakaway from NUPPO and which was forbidden by its constitution from affiliation to or association with any other trade union of political organisation (16). In Glasgow, the police had proposed a minimum wage for constables of £3 per week and a pension after 26 years service, demands which were agreed to by the Secretary of State for Scotland only weeks before the Forty Hours Strike and which no doubt helped to ensure the loyalty of the police during that period. (See pp. 51-2). A further rise to £3 10/- was recommended a few months later by the Desborough Committee which had been set up in 1918 to examine all aspects of policing including the grievances. The Police Act 1919 which gave effect to some of Desborough's recommendations declared unlawful any police trade union and laid down heavy penalties for inciting 'disaffection' within the police force (an offence which remains in section 42 of the Police (Scotland) Act 1967) and established a 'representative' body, the Scottish Police Federation, which was expressly forbidden from affiliating to the TUC.

Internally, the period from Desborough to the end of the Second World War was primarily one of increasing centralisation of the police and the continued adaptation of technical science to police work. The Scottish Police Gazette which circulated throughout the police the names of wanted persons was finally started in 1934 although it had been recommended by the Inspector of Constabulary since the 1860s and an English equivalent had existed since the late nineteenth century, and chief constables began to meet regularly in district conferences in 1939, about 20 years after the practice had been established in England. The Desborough Committee had recommended in 1920 an increase in the central government grant for police forces to 50 per cent of the total, a move which allowed, in the long term, increased direction and control from central government through the Inspector of Constabulary and the regular circulars from the Secretary of State.

In Glasgow, the force was drastically reorganised on the appointment as chief constable of Percy Sillitoe, later to become head of MI5. Sillitoe established a fingerprint and photographic department in 1932, the first police radio transmitter in the city in 1933, and, after he had returned from an international police conference in Chicago, radio cars in 1934. A criminal records office was formally established in 1934.

During the same period the police were considerably involved in the direct repression of working class activity whether it was in the shape of the general strike or in the unemployed workers' movement, the measures of 1919/20 ensuring police loyalty. In the general strike of 1926 the main activity of the police (assisted by the special constables, see pp.47-8), was the escorting of vehicles driven by strike breaking volunteers, and there were innumerable baton charges by the police against the strikers, followed by mass arrests which often resulted in imprisonment with hard labour. One participant in the strike recalls that the police were not always in uniform and that one tactic was simply to chalk mark the back of a striker's coat so that he could be identified and arrested at a later stage (17).

In the thirties the National Unemployed Workers Movement had extensive support throughout Scotland and regular demonstrations took place in all major Scottish towns. These were the objects of various degrees of police action but probably none met with a more violent response than that in Glasgow in 1931 when the police attempted to ban a demonstration through the city centre on October 1st. As the march was forming mounted police and others on foot charged with drawn batons causing an unknown number of injuries. The incident led to questions in parliament the next day about the police action yet the episode was repeated the same day. An historian of the Glasgow force noted that 'For about two years afterwards, policemen patrolling beats in the poorer districts of the city were often jeered at, a practice which ended only when the employment situation began to improve.' (18) Later, Percy Sillitoe, the chief constable of the time was to note how useful his police box system and introduction of police cars had been in controlling similar demonstrations.(19)

During the war years the duties of the police expanded to take in questions of internal security, their role no better expressed than by the orthodox historian of the English police: 'they acted throughout the war as a kind of intelligence service, reporting... on the state of public order and civilian morale... the effect of enemy propaganda, and signs of industrial unrest. Mingling with the ordinary population, they were uniquely placed to report on matters of this kind.' (20)

In Scotland, daily intelligence reports were supplied to central government by the police in every urban centre in addition to those supplied on a similarly regular basis by Special Branch.

In a relatively short space of time then a new police system had been formed to replace a system which was no longer adequate to changed social and economic conditions. In general, it was not seen as a hostile force by those whom it was supposed to police and it had achieved a certain degree of efficiency, uniformity of standards and, although maintained on a local basis, was nevertheless subject to extensive control and direction from central government. It is important to situate this new police in the overall context where the state, by the end of the nineteenth century, had encroached on more and more areas of social and political life especially through the criminal law and the criminal justice system generally. The development of the police was not only of many ways in which the state sought to maintain 'order' and enforce norms, it was equally important one of the ways in which it sought also to legitimate itself.

NOTES

1. For a description of social conditions in Scotland at this time see Hobsbawm, especially page 264; 'Scots wage rates remained on the whole much below the English level throughout the nineteenth century. The mid-Victorian growth industries had a tradition of harshness and compulsion (until 1799 Scots miners were actually serfs)... Scots housing was and remains not only scandalously bad, but notably worse than English housing. Moreover, the squalor and dirt which came with industrial expansion, which was merely awful in the semi-rural mining settlements, became dangerous in the slightly superior but nevertheless appalling

prison cells of the vast and sombre tenement blocks which grew up in the raw smoky fog of Glasgow... The traditional institutions of pre-industrial Scotland such as the education system lost their effectiveness in the industrial society. They broke down in the 1840s, which saw the end of the old Scots poor-relief system and the Disruption of the Kirk... if the mid-Victorian years were a gloomy age in the social life of the English poor, they were a black one in Scotland.'

2. Royal Burghs (Scotland) Act.
3. Mathieson, p. 187.
4. Reith, p. 206.
5. Mather, p. 130.
6. Bunyan, p. 64.
7. Bunyan, p. 65.
8. List, p. 21.
9. List, appendix.
10. see, for example, Prebble, p. 128.
11. quoted in Richards, p. 110, n. 13.
12. Prebble, p. 67.
13. Johnston, p. 337.
14. Grant, p. 29.
15. Bunyan, p. 68-69.
16. Scottish Police Federation, p. 16-17.
17. Kibblewhite and Rigby, p. 20.
18. Grant, p. 97.
19. Sillitoe, p. 154-5.
20. Critchley, p. 232-3, quoted in Bunyan, p. 71.

PART TWO

POLICING TODAY

1. Structure of the Scottish Police

Since 1945 the number of separate police forces in Scotland has been considerably reduced although recommendations for greater centralisation had been made since the 1920s and 30s. The 1933 Police Consolidation Committee, for example, had recommended a reduction from 48 forces to 14. In 1945 there were 49 forces in Scotland, in 1950 there were 33, and in 1968 there were 22. But the most important stage in this centralisation came with the reorganisation of Scottish local government in May 1975 (1). This reduced the number of forces to the present 8. Six of these cover areas governed by a single regional authority, while two cover more than one authority— Northern which takes in Highlands Region, the Western Isles, Orkney and Shetland; and Lothian and Borders. The forces range from Strathclyde which has an actual strength of 6,352 police officers and is the largest force outside the London Metropolitan area covering just under half of Scotland's population of 5 million and the greater part of its industrial heartland, to Dumfries and Galloway, the smallest force in Scotland with an actual strength of 292. (See map on page 35 and chart on page 36).

As the number of separate forces has been reduced the number of officers has greatly increased. In 1945 the authorised strength of the police was 7,200 in Scotland. In 1978 it was 13,144, an increase of around 85%. In the same period the population of Scotland has increased by only a few per cent. The increase in strength is actually greater than these figures show, for at the same time as establishments have increased, the number of civilian staff employed by the police has also increased considerably.(2) In 1960, the police civilian staff was only 913, by 1968 the figure had risen to 1,638, and by the end of 1978 there were over 3,000 people employed by the police, and this figure was 1,000 under strength. Civilian staff range from cleaners and domestic staff to computer operators, radio technicians and photographers, and the process of 'civilianisation' along with the coming of the traffic warden system in the mid 1960's has freed police officers from many administrative and technical duties.

From force to force there is considerable variation in the ratio of police officers to population: Central Scotland: 539:1, Dumfries and Galloway 482:1; Fife 519:1; Grampian 522:1; Lothian and Borders 363:1; Northern 453:1; Strathclyde 353:1; Tayside 437:1. This pattern follows that of the rest of the United Kingdom where the ratio is lower in the urban and industrial areas.

Each force has the same basic internal structure and organisation. (see figure 3). It is commanded by a chief constable who has from one to seven assistant chief constables (although Dumfries and Galloway has none) one of whom will also be deputy chief constable, each having his own area(s) of responsibility e.g. traffic, crime, administration and personnel, etc. Administration, traffic, communications and criminal records departments are all based at Regional Headquarters as is the regional Special Branch force. Below the level of Headquarters the region is divided into a number of geographical divisions, usually designated by a single letter of the alphabet (it is this letter plus a number which the uniformed officer wears on his shoulder), each division generally having its own administration and Criminal Investigation Branch (CID). A division is usually run by an officer of the rank of superintendent or in the larger forces, chief superintendent, and is further divided into several 'areas'. Finally, each area contains a number of police offices where the officer in charge will be an inspector. Operating across force boundaries and not part of any one force is the Scottish Crime Squad which is made up of detective officers seconded from all Scottish forces. This squad and the CID are dealt with in the next section.

Within the overall structure of the Scottish police the Glasgow force, and now Strathclyde, has always appeared to play a dominant role. Historically, the Glasgow police were always in advance of other forces in Scotland (and sometimes Britain) in terms of specialised development or the adaptation of scientific techniques and technology to policing. This has continued to be the case in the post war years—Glasgow maintained a criminal records office for Scotland on an informal basis until the Scottish Criminal Records Office was formally established in 1960; the first of the four Scottish regional crime squads was based on Glasgow; and the first flying squad in Scotland was formed within the Glasgow force as was the first support unit/special patrol group. In addition, Glasgow always provided training facilities for other forces and Strathclyde continues to do this in specialised areas, for example, drugs.

Furthermore, Glasgow/Strathclyde has always provided extra specialised personnel to assist other forces and this continues to be done today, as for example, in the seven or eight detective officers who until 1979 were seconded to assist Dumfries and Galloway ports unit (3). In a sense then, Glasgow/Strathclyde, as the oldest, largest and geographically the most important police force in Scotland has played the role of informal police headquarters in Scotland, mirroring that played by Scotland Yard in relation to England, indeed to Britain. This is not to disregard the jealously guarded autonomy of other forces but simply to point out that the influence and informal power of Glasgow/Strathclyde has always been considerable. Furthermore, it is a position which continues today in that while successive amalgamations have got rid of the absurdly small forces the size of forces at the other end of the scale has also increased and thus Strathclyde is not only responsible for policing almost half of Scotland's population but also comprises over half of its total police strength. The influence and informal control exercised by the chief constable of Strathclyde within the police service and among police chiefs as a first among equals continues to be considerable. So too is he seen by those outside as the most important representative of the police.

Atomic Energy Police

Although the Atomic Energy Authority Police is numerically very small, no more than 400 throughout the United Kingdom, it is of considerable importance for a number of reasons.

Firstly, the force is quite separate from all other forces in the country, and has no notional accountability to a local police authority. Its accountability lies instead to the Atomic Energy Authority, a nationalised industry board, by which its officers are employed. The board itself is accountable to the Secretary of State for Energy but he has only limited powers over the Authority's administration and is not answerable to parliament for their day to day activities. He may issue directions 'general or particular in character' to the authority but he may not intervene in the detail of its operations except where the national interest so requires.(4)

Secondly, it has more extensive powers than other police forces. Its original powers were defined under the Special Constabulary Act 1923 which permitted the guarding of military 'yards and stations' and a fifteen mile radius thereof, but the Atomic Energy Authority (Special Constables) Act 1976 created new powers including the right to carry arms at all times, to engage in hot pursuit of thieves of nuclear material and to arrest on suspicion. The limit of the fifteen mile radius was also removed.

At present, the Atomic Energy Authority Constabulary's main task in Scotland is the guarding of the experimental fast breeder reactor at Dounreay in Caithness and the experimental reactor at Chapelcross in the Borders, but it is also responsible for guarding movements of nuclear material, especially plutonium, which is regularly moved from the Windscale plant in Cumbria to Dounreay. "7 Days" reported in January 1978 that shipments were moved each week by road in armed convoy (5). If the development of the nuclear energy programme continues then the size of the AEA Constabulary must necessarily increase. It is impossible to be specific about the extent of such an increase but Flood and Grove-White, in their study of the civil liberty implications of nuclear power, postulate a reference year when there exist 50 fast breeder reactors and 50 light water reactors in the U.K. and make a 'modest guess at the scale of a future constabulary... of 5000 armed men', although they point out: 'We should emphasise we have no authority for this figure'.(6) But they also point out that the AEA Constabulary has no remit to guard property of the electricity generating authorities, in Scotland principally the South of Scotland Electricity Board (SSEB), so that if the SSEB came to operate its own fast breeder reactor it would presumably require its own police force with similar powers to those of the AEA police.

NOTES

1. Local Government (Scotland) Act 1973.
2. Some, but by no means all or even a majority, of this increased personnel has been made necessary by a shortening of the police working week, longer holidays, increased training etc. See, for example, 'Where have all the (Scottish) PCs gone?' by Quintin Wilson, Police Review, 11.4.80.
3. see page
4. Atomic Energy Act 1954, s. 3.
5. 20.1.78.
6. Flood and Grove-White, p. 19.

Figure 1: Scotland's police force areas.
[Northern includes Orkney and Shetland which are not shown]

Force	Head-quarters	Population [1,000s]	Strength auth.	actual	Pop Per* Police Officer	Special Branch**	Special Constabulary
Central Scotland Police	Stirling	272	505	409	539	5	215
Dumfries and Galloway Constabulary	Dumfries	143	29	29	482	3	248
Fife Constabulary	Kirkcaldy	339	653	625	519	6	348
Grampian Police	Aberdeen	459	880	856	522	8	393
Lothian and Borders Police	Edinburgh	85	2,361	2,151	363	23	451
Northern Constabulary	Inverness	258	569	575	453	3***	333
Strathclyde Police	Glasgow	2,466	6,977	6,352	353	69	833
Tayside Police	Dundee	402	920	908	43	9	317
TOTAL		5,196	13,162	12,223	395 (Av.)	126	3,138

* Based on actual force strengths

** Based on estimate of 1 per cent of authorised strength

*** Actual official Figure 1979

Figure 2: Police Forces in Scotland [1978 figures unless otherwise stated]

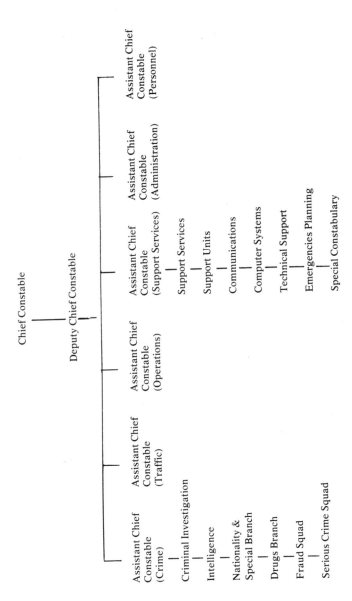

Figure 3: Structure of Strathclyde Police

2. Detective Branches and Pre-emptive Policing

The gathering of criminal intelligence has probably always been seen as an essential part of policing. What is new is first-ly, the extent to which such intelligence is gathered today and, secondly, the sophistication of the ways in which material is collated, stored and eventually used. In the past, intelligence would have been collected on an informal and casual basis, stored, if at all, on manual records, but more often simply held in the head of a particular police officer. Today, each police force has a number of police officers specifically assigned to the gathering of criminal intelligence which is channelled to a central collator at headquarters. In addition, each branch of the detective force will have its own specific interest in in-telligence material.

Intelligence is essentially concerned with those whom the police believe are **likely** to commit offences either because they have done so in the past and/or because they belong to one of a number of groups whose activities, the police assume, will eventually run counter to the law. In the first case lies the im-portance to the police of maintaining criminal records; in the second lies the **raison d'etre** for much of the activities of drugs squads, crime squads, and, of course, the Special Branch, which is almost completely concerned with surveillance, the policing of ideas as opposed to activity, and the notion of pre-emptive policing. While it may be argued that intelligence is essential to some degree to efficient policing, the assumption on which it is based runs counter to the 'presumption of innocence' on which the Scottish (and English) legal system is supposed to be based. In any case, the notion has been used to extend the net of surveillance to cover far more people and organisations than would otherwise have been **legitimately possible.**

A rare view of police intelligence methods was given in 1979 when file cards lost by a detective in South London were shown to a journalist. He reported: 'They show that police regularly record gossip, hearsay and unsubstantiated information; that they permanently file details of any type of police activity against an individual, irrespective of any charge or conviction; and that they open and update files on people who have never been convicted or even suspected of any criminal offence' (1). Similar records are maintained by police forces throughout the country although their sophistication and extent may vary with the resources available and the particular interests of the collator of 'local intelligence officer'. It should be emphasised that this kind of intelligence gathering is **routine** and additional to the more specific work carried out by specialised detective branches.

Since the end of the Second World War all Scottish police forces have maintained a branch of detective officers although many had not done so prior to this. These branches vary in strength but comprise on average 9 per cent of the total number of officers in the force. The detective force generally includes an enquiry and identification branch and will also include a number of officers concerned primarily with gathering criminal intelligence information channelled to a central collator at headquarters. The larger forces may also include separate sections dealing with serious crime (e.g. murder), vice, nationality and the registration of aliens, and stolen vehicles. The officer commanding the CID will generally be of the rank of Superintendent or Chief Superintendent.

Drugs

Six of the Scottish forces have full time drugs squads while the remaining two have 'drugs liaison officers'. According to the Chief Inspector of Constabulary: 'There is a regular exchange of information between officers in the regions and the Central Drugs Intelligence Unit in London'. And in addition, that: 'Efforts to control the situation by drugs squad officers have involved surveillance on those known **or suspected** of using drugs' (2).

The Drugs Intelligence Unit referred to is based at New Scotland Yard and is part of the Metropolitan Police. It was set up in 1972 (along with the Illegal Immigration Intelligence Unit) (3): its purpose, according to a Home Office press release: 'to receive, collate, evaluate and disseminate information relating to known **or suspected** offenders' (4). Although it began with the 18,000 records held by the Metropolitan Police it is now believed to hold over a quarter of a million names, constituting a **national** record of known and suspected offenders. These records have now been transferred to the Metropolitan Police Criminal Intelligence Computer System which is dealt with in Chapter 5.

Scottish Crime Squad

The structure of local CIDs and their specialist branches is supplemented by a Scottish Crime Squad which works across force boundaries and to which officers from all Scottish forces are seconded. The squad was formed in 1969 replacing the four Scottish regional crime squads which had been set up between 1960 and 1969. The purpose of the squad, which is based in Glasgow with branch offices elsewhere in Scotland and which is controlled by a committee of chief constables chaired by the chief constable of Strathclyde, is to assist all Scottish police forces in the prevention and detection of serious crime especially where more than one police area is involved, and to collect, collate and disseminate criminal intelligence to the extent necessary for the work of the squad' (5). The squad's main target is 'travelling criminals' and in 1978 its investigations, although primarily of theft, included murder, possession of explosives, fraud and drugs (6). Its current strength is 40 officers (10 under authorised strength) and it has at its disposal 18 vehicles. Officers train along with members of the nine Regional Crime Squads in England and Wales which have been operational since 1965 and in 1978 much of its success was attributed to its undercover work assisted by a new communications system developed by police scientific experts at the Scottish Home and Health Department. The Commander of the squad told the press that the compact system was a 'technical breakthrough' (7).

Many officers apparently believe, however, that the Scottish Crime Squad is no longer necessary now that forces are larger and capable of greater specialisation and when many have their own specialist serious crimes squads. The Scottish Crime Squad, they argue, has outlived any usefulness it might have had and should now be disbanded. This attitude is reflected in the reluctance of regional forces to invite the Scottish Crime Squad to assist them in their investigations (8).

Scottish Criminal Records Office

As noted earlier the City of Glasgow police had maintained a criminal records office (CRO) for the whole of the country on an informal basis until 1960 when the Scottish Criminal Records Office (SCRO) was formally established. The SCRO continues to be situated in Glasgow at the headquarters of Strathclyde police. The SCRO is linked both to Scotland Yard CRO and to regional CROs in England and Wales. It holds 750,000 entries relating to criminal convictions and offences, 45,000 entries on a photographic index and 291,000 entries on the main index of fingerprints.

In 1976 a working party was set up to investigate the computerisation of the records and reported in 1977 that such computerisation was both 'feasible and essential'. A Project Team was established in 1978 of the police, SCRO, Scottish Office and Home Office representatives and recommended a pilot scheme involving the transfer of Dumfries and Galloway records to the computer facilities of Tayside Police. This will make it possible for information to be shown on visual display units (VDUs) at divisional headquarters. The cost of the scheme is being borne by the Scottish Home and Health Department.

Access to criminal records is supposed to be limited to serving police officers and information should only be supplied to the courts or the prison service 'but otherwise the principle is that no record information is given to anyone, however res-

ponsible, unless considerations of public interest justify it'.
(9) Reports about current convictions are however made by
the police to the relevant public or professional body about a
number of people including doctors, dentists, those working
with young people, those working in the courts and the legal
profession, those employed in the Post Office, civil service and
the atomic energy industry. It is clear, however, that access
and disclosure are not limited in this way. A number of
employers use private tracing agencies to obtain information/
on potential employees. These agencies frequently employ ex-
police officers who appear to experience little difficulty in
obtaining the information sought. 'The vulnerability of these
offices (CROs) is especially great to former members of the
police, who are invariably well versed in the techniques of
making such requests. Industrial firms employ retired policemen in large numbers as security officers, precisely because
of their familiarity with police routines in these or other matters. In many cases too, the personal ties between these private security officers and their former colleagues make it possible for them to obtain services which would be denied to
others'.(10) In addition, there is evidence that there is a connection between police records and the 'information service',
supplied by the Economic League, which is used to vet potential employees and weed out 'militants' and 'subversives'.
'An ex-employee of the League's Glasgow office described
how prospective employers would be advised against hiring
on the grounds that the employee had a previous criminal
record'.(11)

The vulnerability of CROs to this kind of illegal access is
increased when they are computerised and especially when
the computer facilities are not under the sole control of the
police. The facilities used by Tayside Police for example are
time shared on a computer under the control of Tayside Regional Council. In addition, the dangers to individuals of
unlawful access are increased by the practice of including
with criminal records suspicions or other non-factual remarks.
Since criminal records are normally maintained until the subject is dead or has reached retirement a person who may have
committed no more than one or two minor offences when

young will be subject to a file which may contain information which is inaccurate, unfounded or irrelevant but which cannot be corrected or removed because s/he does not know of it.

NOTES

1. New Statesman, 10.8.79.
2. Annual Report for 1977, emphasis added.
3. For information on this unit see State Research Bulletin No. 10.
4. Quoted in Bunyan, p. 83-84, emphasis added.
5. Her Majesty's Chief Inspector of Constabulary for Scotland, Annual Report for 1975.
6. The Scotsman, 6.6.78.
7. The Scotsman, 9.6.78.
8. See Glasgow Herald, 8.3.80
9. Computers, Safeguards for Privacy Cmnd. 6354, (HMSO 1975), para. 39.
10. Rule, p. 82, quoted in Bunyan, p. 81.
11. The Guardian, 29.6.78. (Quoted in State Research Bulletin No. 7).

3. Special Patrol Groups and the Special Constabulary

Although attention has recently focussed on the activities of the Special Patrol Group (SPG) in London most people remain unaware that at least two police forces in Scotland have their own version of this special para-military squad. The Strathclyde Support Unit was originally part of the City of Glasgow Police and was formed in April 1973 by the then chief constable, David McNee. Central Scotland police's support unit was formed some years later. (Although no other Scottish chief constable reports on the existence of a similar group it is likely that they do exist, especially in some of the larger forces for example in Lothian and Borders or Grampian. Nationally, there are known to be SPG-type groups in just under half of the police forces in the U.K. although they frequently carry different titles, for example, commando unit, task force, etc.) (1).

SPGs were largely formed in response to the debate around the question of whether Britain needed a 'third force', that is a para-military police force, similar to that which exists in most European countries (for example, the French CRS) whose function lies between that of the police and the military. Public opinion has always been hostile to suggestions that Britain should have such a force and this was recognised by a Home Office working party which had been set up in 1961 to examine the issue. Reporting secretly ten years later, the working party recommended that instead of creating a new force 'existing police forces should be retrained and re-equipped to fill the gaps that existed' (2). The conclusions of the working party were repeated and extended by the National Security Committee, which had been formed by the Tory government in

1972 following the miners' strike of the same year. The NSC recommended a drastic revision of police training in riot control and the use of firearms and the holding of regular joint police-military exercises. Clear lines were to be laid down about the use of the army and plain clothes units of the Special Air Service regiment (SAS) should be held on permanent standy-by for any situation the police could not handle (3).

But SPGs were also a response to the development in urban areas of what is now known as 'fire brigade' policing, where the police rush to trouble spots and incidents as distinct from providing regular street patrols, and their forerunners can be seen in the police 'mobile units' which operated in Dunbartonshire near Glasgow in the 1960s and in Glasgow's own mobile squad known colloquially as the 'Untouchables' or 'touchies' who carried out a policy of aggressive policing in the city's working class areas. In April 1973 the first Support Unit was formally established in Glasgow.

The Support Unit consisted of specially selected uniformed officers under the command of the Assistant Chief Constable (Operations) and numbered 36: 1 inspector, 3 sergeants and 32 constables— equipped with one 12 seater personnel carrier. The unit was based in the north of the city and was described by McNee in his report for the year as being 'highly trained and well officered, free to give immediate attention to any serious problem in all areas of the city' (4). Another unit was set up six months later in the south side of the city with similar strength and a chief inspector put in day to day command. McNee concluded his remarks on the unit: 'I am satisfied that the Support Unit has proved its worth and has created a splendid image of the force to the public'.

In 1977, following the reorganisation of the force management, the Support Units became the responsibility of the Assistant Chief Constable (Support Services) whose other responsibilities include the special constabulary, technical support services and emergency planning. (See diagram on page 37). Along with the dogs and mounted branches, the river patrol and underwater units, the Support Unit has divisional status under a chief superintendent.

There are now five sections within the Support Unit, situated at Springburn and Pollockshaws on the north and south sides respectively of Glasgow and in the nearby towns of Renfrew, Motherwell and Kilmarnock. The total strength at the end of 1977 was 120 constables, 19 sergeants and 5 inspectors and the total number of arrests made by the unit during the year was over 5,000. Officers are all volunteers with four or five years experience and serve with the unit for two years. (There are usually two volunteers for each vacancy).

Central Scotland police are also known to have a Support Unit although no details of strength or composition are given. The purpose of the unit, according to the chief constable is 'to combat crime, provide additional strength for major enquiries, missing person searches and other contingencies' (5).

It is the fire brigade policing which has dominated the use of SPGs in Scotland, and in other parts of the country they have a reputation for aggressive policing, reflected in their high arrest rates and the number of complaints made about their behaviour and attitudes to solicitors and others if not through the formal police complaints mechanism.

The units however remain essentially a para-military force to be used in that capacity as necessary. All members are trained in the use of firearms—according to a senior police officer: 'They are all expert marksmen, from the ordinary constables to the Chief Inspectors.'(6) And, according to the same report, are believed to be the only officers who are trained to any extent in the use of rifles. They also receive training in crowd control, i.e. riot training and rescue from buildings. Their work includes large scale searches, house to house enquiries, road blocks, etc. and they are present at a variety of public occasions from football matches to political demonstrations. Indeed, the Strathclyde Support Unit first came to the public's attention when in May 1975 it was used to break up a demonstration blocking the entrance to a hall booked for a National Front meeting. Over 100 people were arrested including several prominent local trade unionists— half of whom were eventually acquitted. A call for a public inquiry into the police action, supported by the Scottish TUC, was refused.

A completely different role to that played by the Support Units is that of the Special Constabulary, the voluntary police reserve force. While the one is a highly specialised squad drawn from the regular police the other exists primarily to assist the police in times of emergency and may only perform a few hours of duty each month on ordinary police work. This usually involves assisting the regular police at sporting events or other public occasions and on beat patrols, although in Edinburgh, for example, specials also perform plain clothes duties using their own cars for which they receive a petrol allowance.

The forerunners of the specials can be seen in the power of J.P.s and parish constables in the seventeenth century to swear in certain 'better class' citizens for a period usually of one year and in the practice, which continued until the nineteenth century, of conscripting adult males into the Town Guards which patrolled towns and cities at night before the advent of the new police. The importance of the specials declined as they were replaced by regular forces but they continued to be used in emergencies. In Glasgow in 1848, 10,000 specials were sworn in within two days for use against Chartist demonstrators and the specials were regularly called out at election times. In the twentieth century, the War Cabinet in 1919 considered the use of specials to break the Forty Hours Strike, the Clydeside mass movement for a shorter working week without loss of wages.(7) The cabinet, aware that the local troops could not be relied upon to turn their guns upon their fellow workers believed the specials to be more reliable, but, given the strength of the movement, mobilised English and Highland troops and moved them into Glasgow. In 1926, during the General Strike, over 1,300 people volunteered as specials in Glasgow and were used mainly to provide escorts for those who continued to work. The Earl of Glasgow had previously offered the Scottish Office the use of over 2,000 members of fascist organisations as specials. There was some official disquiet about this and the men were eventually advised by the authorities that if they wished they could enrol as individuals in the strike breaking Organisation for the Maintenance of Supplies.(8) In Edinburgh, 'The

Scotsman' (which continued to be published during the strike) said: 'It is doubtful if the citizens as a body will ever realise what they owe to the Special Constables in the disturbances...'(9)

Until 1956, the specials in Scotland were technically an emergency, and not an auxiliary, force and they could only be used in an emergency or when necessary to prevent or suppress riot. (This was a more restricted role than that of the English special.) The restrictions were criticised from a number of sides including the Police Post War Committee and the Inspector of Constabulary argued in successive reports that the restrictions seriously affected recruitment. (In 1945 the strength of the special constabulary in Scotland stood at 7,000 but began to decline in the 1950s.) In 1956 the use of specials on ordinary duties was permitted for the first time, so long as they themselves consented(10). The change, however, did little to increase recruitment as had been hoped. Indeed, many specials resented the remaining restrictions on the maximum number of hours they were permitted to work and the introduction of a special insignia indicating that the bearer was a member of the Special Constabulary and not a regular police officer, and membership continued to fall. The introduction of new regulations and conditions in 1966 reduced the membership by almost 2,000 and a further 600 have been lost since. The actual strength now stands at around 3,100, about one third of the authorised establishment, and in his report for 1976, the Chief Inspector of Constabulary noted that if the trend were to continue the special constabulary would be extinct by the 1980s. However, it is likely, that while the special constabulary may have few attractions in normal times, in periods of unrest or threats to the established social order significant numbers of people, probably drawn from those most threatened by such changes, will be found as they have been in the past to join the specials and play their part in upholding the status quo.

NOTES

1. See State Research Bulletin No. 13 for a survey of, and background information on, SPGs in Britain.

2. ibid.

3. ibid.

4. Annual Report for 1973, p. 108.

5. Annual Report for 1977.

6. Glasgow Herald, 12.12.78.

7. See also page

8. Scottish Records Office, HH1/35.

9. 22.5.26.

10. Police (Scotland) Act 1956.

4. The Special Branch

Of all the branches of the police, the Special Branch, which is part of the detective branch, is most closely connected with political activity and political ideas. It is responsible for the investigation of offences against the state, most commonly those in connection with official secrets or under anti-terrorist laws, but for the most part it is engaged on other duties. In particular it works on the basis of pre-emption discussed earlier (see pp. 38-9) investigating not those who may have committed offences but those whom it believes will do so at some future point. As we shall see the range of such persons and organisations is largely defined by the Special Branch itself using the vague definitions and extensive discretion allowed to it by parliament.

The Special Branch in Scotland 1883-1961

The Special Branch was formed in 1883 as the Special Irish Branch to deal with bombings by the Fenian Irish Nationalists in Britain. It was essentially a London based branch of the police until the 1960s when provincial forces began to establish their own Special Branches. Until then Special Branch enquiries in the provinces were carried out by CID officers who, depending on the level of work, might be seconded to Special Branch duties. In Scotland, it is likely that a standing Special Branch existed in Glasgow because of the area's political and industrial importance and because of the relationship of the Glasgow police force to other Scottish forces (see pp. 31-32) In any case the events which led to the formation of the Special Branch in London were mirrored in Scotland. In 1883 a local offshoot of the Fenian Brotherhood, the Ribbon Society, was active in Glasgow and was responsible for explosions at a gasworks and at a railway station before nine members of the Society were arrested and convicted after a police investigation involving co-operation with the police in London and Antwerp.

By the early twentieth century the Special Branch's attention had switched to local socialists and the anti-war movement, especially on Clydeside. Plain clothes police officers regularly attended political meetings and their reports and evidence led to the prosecution of prominent figures in the labour movement, including John Maclean who was convicted three times in as many years; in 1915 under the sweeping Defence of the Realm Act when he was sent to prison for five days for refusing to pay a fine; in 1916 for sedition—for speaking out against the war; and again in 1917, after his appointment as Soviet Consul in Glasgow and amidst a 'red scare', again for breaches of the Defence of the Realm Act. During the same period various socialist papers, Vanguard, Forward and The Worker were suppressed by the government, the latter two for printing an account of a rowdy meeting between Prime Minister Lloyd George and the Clyde Workers Committee, and other prominent socialists were imprisoned, including Willie Gallacher and James Maxton on sedition charges. Harry MacShane recalls that Gallacher and others 'were charged with publishing an article called "Should the Workers Arm?". In fact, the unsigned article was written by Willie Reagan of the Catholic Socialist Society, and it was against insurrection and argued that the workers should not arm. But, for the government, the title was enough'.(1) The official concern, amounting to panic, at what was happening on Clydeside and elsewhere came to a head in 1919 with the Forty Hours Strike which culminated in the mobilisation of troops in Glasgow and on Friday 31st January, a police baton charge on strikers in the city's main square. Even the Glasgow Herald, a paper totally and vigorously hostile to the strike was moved to comment: 'with a vigour and determination that was a prelude to the extraordinary scenes which the Square was afterwards to witness, and to which the city, with all its acquaintance with labour troubles, can happily offer no parallel. A strong body of police... swept the crowd in front of them, raining a hurricane of blows which fell indiscriminately on those actually participating in the strike and on those who had been drawn to the scene merely through curiosity.'(2) Bloody Friday, as it came to be known, was followed by the prosecution of four prominent strikers, Gallacher, David Kirkwood, Emanuel Shinwell (then chairman of the Glasgow Trades Council) and Harry Hopkins, and eight others, on charges of rioting and incitement to riot. Reviewing official reactions to the events of the period a contemporary historian has ascribed much of it to the 'excitable and alarmist' intelligence reports being submitted to the War Cabinet by the head of Special Branch, Basil Thomson, in his 'Fortnightly Reports on Revolutionary Organisations in the United Kingdom, and Morale in Foreign Countries'—'...the quality of the information he supplied to the War Cabinet was often disastrously bad. It sometimes differed from the 'red scares' of the popular press only in being printed on paper headed 'This Document is the Property of His Britannic Majesty's Government.'(3)

Thomson himself believed that 'The plan of the revolutionary minority was to use the Clyde as the touchstone of a general strike, and, if it proved to be successful, to bring out the engineers and the railways all over the country, to seize the food and to achieve a revolution. The scheme failed... It is now known that during the disorder on Friday January 31st, the intention was to seize the Municipal Buildings in Glasgow, but the police were too strong for them'.(4) Suffice to say that such a view is not at all shared by those closely involved in the strike, including both Gallacher and Harry MacShane. The latter says 'We regarded the Forty Hours Strike not as a revolution but as a beginning. Other things would follow: it was the first rank-and-file agitation to be led by socialists after the war.'(5)

In the twenties the interests of the Branch were mainly threefold. The Irish, the Communist Party (which had been founded in 1920) and the National Unemployed Workers Movement (NUWM). In 1922, the year of the establishment of the Irish Free State, the Chief of the Imperial General Staff was assassinated in London and the two Sinn Fein Members responsible arrested and executed. Responding to criticism for allowing this to happen the Branch set about updating its records on the Irish in Britain and illegally deported one hundred members of Irish political groups in Britain.(6) The index to Scottish Home Department records shows the existence of extensive reports on Irish Republicanism and 'Irish disturbances' from 1920 until 1923.(7)

The formation in 1920 of the Communist Party meant that there was yet another group which required surveillance as did, in official eyes, the NUWM. An examination of police records for England and Wales for this period has shown extensive infiltration by the police of the movement between 1929-35. It would be reasonable to suppose that this was repeated in Scotland. Again the index to official police records shows that local forces submitted regular reports on the activities of the unemployed groups from 1931 until the commencement of war in 1939.(8) In any case, plain clothes police officers attended meetings of the unemployed. In Glasgow two were discovered at an open air meeting on Glasgow Green in 1932 and only the arrival of uniformed police prevented their being thrown into the river Clyde.(9) The idea, generally held by the police at this time, that the NUWM was a 'front' for, or heavily 'infiltrated' by, the Communist Party was also shared by Glasgow's chief constable, Percy Sillitoe, at this time. In his autobiography he wrote: 'Glasgow's mass unemployment made the city a fertile breeding ground for Communist propaganda, and the Communists were never averse to taking advantage of the wretched hopelessness of the unemployed by inflaming their sense of injury and fanning their distress into active, disorderly rebellion which made conditions harder for everyone and did nobody any good.'(10)

At the same time interest in the Irish continued, especially as war with Germany became imminent and in 1936 a detailed report was prepared at the request of the Lord Advocate on the Irish Catholic population in Scotland showing their numbers, distribution, occupations and duration of residence. Such information no doubt proved useful after the IRA bombing campaign in Britain of 1939-40 and the passing of the

Prevention of Violence (Temporary Provisions) Act 1939 which provided extended powers of search, arrest and detention and allowed the Home Secretary to order the deportation of those believed to be connected with the IRA.

Irish nationalists were not the only concern of the Branch at this time and various Scottish nationalists are believed to have been under surveillance. A closed file in the Scottish Records Office indicates the compilation of reports on nationalist organisations by local forces from 1941-43 under the heading of sedition.(11) The official Scottish National Party line at the outbreak of war was that Scotland should fight alongside England but hard-line nationalists in the Scottish Neutrality League opposed Scots involvement in the war. (The German Nazis even established a radio station, Radio Caledonia, in an effort to spread disaffection.) Various nationalists, including pacifists, were arrested while others maintain that they were watched by the police.(12) The various incidents involving raids on the homes of prominent nationalists and the seizure of literature (and occasional arrest) led to questions being asked in parliament by James Maxton, M.P., but not surprisingly, the government denied that anything irregular or untoward had occurred. The file on Maxton's questions and the answers supplied is however one of those which is closed for 100 years.(13) In the 1950s nationalists continued to pose problems for the Branch and it was the Special Branch which was responsible for investigation into the removal of the Stone of Destiny from Westminster Abbey by nationalists in 1950.(14)

The '50s and '60s were key years in the development of the Branch on a national scale. In the Campaign for Nuclear Disarmament, Direct Action and the Committee of 100, it was faced with a huge mass movement which drew its support from all sections of society and from almost every conceivable occupation. The problems of surveillance of such a qualitatively different movement from many of those which had preceded it were insurmountable but were added to in 1963 by the publication of details of the secret Regional Seats of Government (RSGs) by the 'Spies for Peace' including that of the Scottish RSG at Corstorphine Hill, Edinburgh. Despite intense activity by the Branch, including widespread surveillance and raids on the homes of activists, the source of the leak—duplicated in hundreds of different leaflets and pamphlets up and down the country—was never traced.

In the midst of the CND years, in 1961 the Special Branch was internally reorganised. The main effect of this reorganisation was to set up permanent Special Branch squads outside London in provincial forces which would begin by collating and assessing intelligence material already gathered by local police forces. Between 1955 and 1961 the number of Branch officers in Britain had risen from 150 to about 220. After the changes of 1961 the total number of Branch officers had risen to around 450.(15)

The Special Branch Today

Special Branch officers are nominally accountable to their own chief constable but usually report direct to Special Branch headquarters at Scotland Yard and, of course, any information supplied by them will be stored on the Branch's computer and will be available to other Branch officers. This belies the notion that there is no national Special Branch force, an idea which has allowed government ministers to avoid questions on Special Branch operations. During a parliamentary debate on the surveillance of the Agee-Hosenball Defence Committee and the arrests of Aubrey, Berry and Campbell on official secrets charges in 1977, Dr. Shirley Summerskill for the Home Office, replying to Robin Cook, M.P., said: 'There is no national Special Branch. Only in the annual report of each chief constable can there be an annual report on individual branches.'(16) However, a survey carried out by State Research a few months previously and covering 36 Chief Constables' Annual Reports (including all eight from Scotland) showed that in only one (Durham) was any information given about the Special Branch.

A second survey in 1979 showed that although a number of chief constables in England and Wales had begun to provide information on the Special Branch, in an effort to legitimate its activities, none of the chief constables in Scotland did so. The Inspector of Constabulary had however in 1977, as a response to the publicity over the Paisley incident, described below, stated that 'Scottish police forces have for many years operated very small units of officers, comprising less than 1% of authorised establishment, on special duties in connection with the security of the State This is necessary to deal with people intent on destroying that security by violent means.' (17) This 1% figure would give approximate Special Branch strengths in Scottish forces as follows:

Central	5
Dumfries and Galloway	3
Fife	6
Grampian	8
Lothian and Borders	23
Northern	5
Strathclyde	69
Tayside	9

giving a total of 128 in Scotland as a whole. This is considerably higher than the figure of 97 given to parliament by the Scottish Office Minister for Home Affairs and the Environment, Malcolm Rifkind, in November 1979,(18), but there are likely to be a number of detective officers seconded to Special Branch work on a temporary basis and who may make up the difference. In the absence of exact figures from the Scottish Office and the chief constables it is not possible to be more precise, but a limited check of the 1% estimate is possible in four cases. Until 1979 Dumfries and Galloway had a ports unit at Stranraer which included four detective officers, who were presumably local Special Branch, supplemented by seven or eight detectives from Strathclyde Police. (Since 1979 the Strathclyde officers have been replaced by local personnel.) In Lothian and Borders local sources indicated that the original estimated Special Branch strength of 14 published by State Research in 1977 was at least 50% too low.(19) Similarly in the case of Strathclyde it was reliably reported that the actual number of Special Branch officers was nearer 60.(20) In the case of the Northern Constabulary the chief constable stated in his report for 1979 that three officers (two sergeants and a constable) were employed full time on

Special Branch duties. He is the only chief constable in Scotland to have provided such information.

Whatever the exact figures there is no doubt that the strength of the Special Branch in Scotland has increased considerably in recent years. Even the figure given in parliament in 1979 was an increase of some 27 or more than one third on the number given in 1978. The question may rightly be asked: what do all these Special Branch officers do? Generally speaking, the Special Branch outside London has five main functions: the supervision of ports and airports, the surveillance of 'subversive' individuals and organisations, the monitoring of aliens, protection duties and 'assisting the uniformed police in the maintenance of order'.(21)

Supervision at Ports and Airports

The supervision of ports and airports, in practice the watching for known or suspected terrorists and 'undesirable' political or criminal elements and the logging of the movements of prominent political activists, has traditionally been a Special Branch function. In Scotland, as elsewhere in Britain, this has taken on even greater significance since the passing in 1974 of the Prevention of Terrorism (Temporary Provisions) Act (PTA). The PTA, which was passed following the Birmingham bombings, gave the police considerably extended powers of search, questioning, arrest and detention. In particular, it allowed for detention at ports of entry (including airports) of up to seven days, with a possible extension of another five days on application to the Secretary of State. Following Lord Shackleton's report on the operation of the act(22) the maximum period of detention at a port was reduced to 48 hours with the possibility of a five day extension on application to the Secretary of State, thus bringing it into line with detention periods at places other than ports.

Supervision at ports is carried out by 'ports units' consisting of Special Branch, seconded CID officers, uniformed officers and civilian searchers. In Scotland the most important are based at Stranraer, a major point of arrival and departure for Northern Ireland, where there is a port unit of eleven CID (some presumably Special Branch) officers, six uniformed officers, and eight civilian searchers; Glasgow Airport; Prestwick International Airport; Dyce Airport (Aberdeen); Turnhouse Airport (Edinburgh) and the new expanded Sumburgh Airport in the Shetlands. The ports units are primarily interested in those with some involvement in Irish politics or simply those who are Irish, but they also include those working in the North Sea Oil developments (which has attracted a significant number of Irish workers) which has assumed a major importance for policing. (This is dealt with in more detail below.) Some indication of the extent of Special Branch activity at ports is provided by statistics relating to the Prevention of Terrorism Act. Up to the end of March 1980, 1,088 persons had been detained in Scotland (4,641 in Britain as a whole) although only seven or eight hundred of those would have been held at ports. Of all British forces Dumfries and Galloway and Strathclyde forces have the third and fourth highest number of detentions respectively. Figures for those charged with offences or served with exclusion orders in Scotland are not available but U.K. figures show that only five per cent of those detained were subsequently served with exclusion orders; approximately one per cent were charged with offences under the Act and about five per cent with other offences. The vast majority were neither excluded, charged or convicted of any crime or offence.(23) The statistics clearly show an interest extending far beyond those possibly involved in terrorist activity. People have been detained and questioned about involvement in the Troops Out Movement as well as their general political affiliations; one prominent activist in the Northern Ireland Trade Union Campaign against Repression was served with an exclusion order at Stranraer banning him from re-entering Britain after addressing a Troops Out meeting in London; journalist Ron MacKay was held at Glasgow Airport for 24 hours on his return from an assignment in Northern Ireland, a copy of an article he had written confiscated and charges for a technical breach of the Act brought (these were later dropped); and one person who had previously worked for an organisation with premises adjacent to those of the Scottish Council for Civil Liberties was held for 24 hours and questioned about the work and resources of SCCL and the political beliefs and affiliations of its staff.(24) In Scotland, as much as in Britain as a whole, the Prevention of Terrorism Act has been used as a legitimate means of gathering low level intelligence and of harrassing anyone Irish, or anyone taking any interest in Irish politics or British involvement in Northern Ireland.

Surveillance of Subversive Organisations

Of crucial importance to an understanding of the Special Branch's work in this respect is the definition of 'subversive' and consequently of who or what is thought worthy of the attentions of the Branch. As Bunyan points out, during the 1950s radical political activity was generally subsumed under the heading of 'communist' but since the late 1960s the terms 'subversive' and 'terrorist' have taken over. In 1963, Lord Denning in his report on the Profumo Affair defined as subversive those people who 'would contemplate the overthrow of government by unlawful means'.(25) This was an officially accepted definition. The definition accepted now however is considerably wider. Subversion is now defined as: 'activities which threaten the safety or wellbeing of the State, and are intended to undermine or overthrow parliamentary democracy by political, industrial or violent means.'(26)

There is an important distinction between these two definitions. Lord Denning's was capable of a clear and precise definition based upon the law. The newer definition is not and is not restricted to activities which are unlawful but permits the surveillance by the police of a wide range of individuals and organisations whose activities are quite within the law. Indeed, this point was made by former Home Secretary Merlyn Rees when he told parliament that 'The Special Branch collects information on those who I think cause problems for the State.'(27)

Included in this definition and therefore subject to some sort of surveillance will be political parties from the Labour Party leftwards, parties of the extreme right, non party political groups, ad hoc campaigns and trade union activists. It will also include Irish organisations and their sympathisers, whether Republican or Loyalist, and sections of the Scottish nationalist movement.

Scotland's 'Irish connection' has always been of considerable importance to the Special Branch as was shown in the brief historical account of the Branch's work but it has taken on a new dimension in the past ten years. Although there has been little violence in Scotland itself there have been a number of isolated bombing incidents including an attempt to blow up the headquarters of the Orange Order in Glasgow shortly after British troops were sent to Northern Ireland. The bomb was defused and an assistant chief constable fearing sectarian warfare contacted newspaper editors asking that the story not be printed. The incident went unreported until 1975.(28) In addition there have been a small number of cases involving the supply of money and arms to Protestant organisations in Northern Ireland.

Scottish republicanism too has posed problems for the Branch and the bombing of oil pipelines by the 'Tartan Army' in 1975 led to the formation of Scotland's first bomb squads in Strathclyde and Lothian and Borders, composed of Special Branch, Serious Crime Squad and CID Officers.(29) Members of the 'Army' were successfully prosecuted in 1976 and in the following years members of an 'Army of the Provisional Government' were convicted of possession of explosives and blowing up two oil pipelines.

These have been exceptional cases but it is not generally realised that the Scottish National Party itself, although opposed to the use of violence for the furtherance of its aims, must come within the current definition of 'subversion' because it stands, almost by definition, for the break up the the British state and it is this state which the Special Branch is supposed to protect.

Information Gathering

Methods of gathering information about organisations and individuals are well documented elsewhere (30) but will include the routine monitoring of political newspapers and other publications, the indexing of names on petitions to parliament and those appearing in the press, attendance at meetings and demonstrations, and the receipt of information from informants.

In the more important cases phones will be tapped and mail opened and the 1980 government White Paper on 'The Interception of Communications in Great Britain'(31) indicated the extent to which this practice in Scotland had increased. In 1967, according to the White Paper, only three warrants for telephone tapping had been issued by the Scottish Office. By 1969 the figure had risen to eight but the dramatic rise came in the 1970s—20 warrants in 1973, 41 in 1975, 52 in 1977, rising to a record 56 in 1979. The official figures show a seven fold increase in ten years and a higher level of surveillance **per capita** than in England and Wales.

Even these figures provide only a partial picture as they take account only of warrants granted by the Secretary of State for Scotland to the police and do not therefore include warrants granted to the Security Service (MI5) which are the responsibility of the Home Secretary nor those granted to the Ministry of Defence Police, the Atomic Energy Authority Police or the Secret Intelligence Service (SIS/MI6).

But on the whole much of Special Branch surveillance work is merely routine and they will often be helped by information routinely collected and passed on by other sections of the police. An alternative bookshop in Edinburgh for example noted the routine visits paid by a uniformed police officer to collect details of activities listed on their notice board.(32)

In 1973 a photographer on the East Kilbride News was asked by his editor to go along to the local branch of the Communist Party and take pictures of the prominent party members. When he questioned the use of this he was told by the editor 'in the strictest confidence' that the pictures were to be sent to the Special Branch for inclusion in their dossier of revolutionaries working in the new town.(33)

In 1977, Dr Henry Drucker of the University of Edinburgh, who had recently completed a study of the breakaway Scottish Labour Party found himself at the centre of a police enquiry over his sources of information. The police were investigating the alleged theft of documents from the SLP offices but, according to Drucker, they were 'at least as interested in the content of allegedly stolen documents as in my method of obtaining them. They seemed to be particularly concerned to know if I had any documents which named individual members of the International Marxist Group who had joined the SLP.'(34)

In 1978, the West Highland Free Press reported that a woman living in North Uist who had complained about people being inconvenienced by military exercises in the area was visited and 'grilled' by two Special Branch officers from Glasgow.(35)

The Paisley Incident

A rare illustration of how the Special Branch works in Scotland (and presumably elsewhere) came in the incident at Paisley College of Technology in November 1977. A first year social sciences student, Robert MacNeill was told at the end of a lecture that the college secretary wished to see him. On arriving at the secretary's office he was directed into another room where, according to a statement written by MacNeill, 'a man, probably aged about 50—55, wearing glasses, civilian suit and tie, was seated behind a desk. He showed me a police identification card. I was surprised and did not see the man's name...He asked me if I was interested in helping the police with secret and confidential information and I asked him what he meant. He asked about my political allegiance and I refused to answer the question...He told me that he had got my name because of my father's job as a civilian driver with Edinburgh City Police...and (I) was suitable because of my clean police record...he offered me financial incentives which would be tax free and told me that I would not be seen publicly with him and that any information I was to give would be treated in strict confidence...He asked me to sign a copy of the Official Secrets Act which he produced so that the conversation would be treated in the strictest confidence. I refused.'(36)

The matter was taken up by the local Labour M.P., Norman Buchan, and by the Board of Governors of the college. Chief Constable Patrick Hamill expressed to Mr. Buchan his 'distress' at the approach and went on to say 'You have my assurance that he (the Special Branch officer) was not acting on my instructions and that he had taken it upon himself to seek out and interview Mr MacNeill. You may want to know that I have issued a directive that such practices must cease forthwith.'(37) Similar assurance was given to the Board of Governors after they had accepted MacNeill's account and had admitted to the Students' Association that the Special Branch officer had visited the college on previous occasions. However, the convenor of the local police committee told the press that she had no plans to raise the issue with the chief constable despite the fact that public money was involved. According to The Scotsman: 'If there had been an increase in Special Branch activity she was sure it was justified.'(38)

The question which was raised but never answered was whether this kind of Special Branch activity was typical or whether it was an isolated instance. It is impossible to answer this question but what can be said is that Paisley College of Technology is neither a particularly large institution nor one noted for its political activity although at the time of the incident the College Students' Association banner had been present on a number of demonstrations. There are other educational institutions in Strathclyde and the rest of Scotland which are of more political significance and on that basis it is possible that similar incidents have occurred elsewhere.

Three months after the Paisley incident an incident of vetting, possibly involving the Special Branch, occurred in Edinburgh where a Lothian Regional councillor, Paul Nolan, was approached by a constituent who had been refused a non-teaching post in the Regional Educational Department after a police check on his background. Councillor Nolan took the matter up with the police and after a further check the man was given the job, but the reason for the initial refusal was still unkown.

Nolan said: 'It could have been a parking offence, involvement with left-wing politics, criminal activities—I just do not know.'(39) A statement from the region's Chief Executive confirming that applicants were not told of the check, that the 'safeguards' rested with the police and 'that the basis of the police check is for any convictions which might make the applicant unsuitable for work with youngsters...on the social work side, police simply supplied information and left the decision to the council officials, but for education posts affected by the scheme **the police supply no information simply a recommendation on the person's suitability.**'(40)

Public Order

The Special Branch's 'public order' functions generally cover their attendance at and surveillance of demonstrations and pickets—in line with the wide definition of subversion. On the occasion of a United Troops Out march in Glasgow (and a strong and hostile counter demonstration) Special Branch officers, said to be armed, mingled with the crowd (41); Special Branch officers video-recorded an anti-fascist demonstration in Glasgow (42); and in 1979 a Lothian Regional councillor called for an inquiry into reports that police had dressed as anti-apartheid demonstrators, carrying placards and wearing badges, protesting at rugby matches involving a South African rugby team.(43)

Monitoring of Aliens

Special Branch officers (or their colleagues in the Nationality Branch) are responsible for the monitoring of aliens (people who are not citizens of the U.K. and Colonies). Aliens have to register with the police and are subject to a number of restrictions which date from the early part of this century.(44) They cannot, for example, take part in trade union activity unless they have been working for a particular firm for two years and heavy penalties are prescribed for aliens who cause 'disaffection' among the armed forces or among civilians. Such activities can lead to deportation or the refusal of British citizenship. The Special Branch not only compiles lists of foreigners who might have to be interned in the event of war but also vet all applications for citizenship. Such vetting includes not only interviewing the applicant but also people supplying character references and friends and neighbours and in this respect considerable power lies with the Special Branch.

Protection Duties

Finally, the Special Branch is responsible for the protection of prominent people. While the Royal Family and senior Cabinet Ministers are guarded by specially trained officers seconded from Scotland Yard the Special Branch in Scotland will be responsible for arranging protection for other senior politicians and visiting dignitaries and presumably for assisting in the protection of the Royal Family and others on their regular visits to Scotland.

CONCLUSION

The problems posed by the Special Branch are therefore at least two-fold. Firstly, there is insufficient information made available about it and its work. Secondly, most of its work is not that of preventing or detecting crime but of policing ideas, ideas which it and its masters regard as 'subversive'. In short, if there is to be a Special Branch then it should operate as openly as is consistent with its proper functions and, more important, should be subject to the most rigorous of controls.(45)

NOTES

1. MacShane, p. 80.
2. 1.2.19.
3. 'Red Clydeside 1915-1919' by Iain MacLean, in Stevenston & Quinault.
4. Quoted in MacLean.
5. MacShane, p. 109.
6. Bunyan, p. 119.
7. Scottish Records Office, HH 55/62-76. This, like many other official files of interest, is closed for 100 years.
8. Scottish Records Office, HH 55/661-707.

9. MacShane, p. 193; Sillitoe, p. 153.
10. Sillitoe, p. 153.
11. Scottish Records Office, HH55/557.
12. Webb, p. 56-58.
13. Scottish Records Office, HH55/558.
14. Grant, p. 197.
15. Bunyan, pp.128-9.
16. Hansard, 5.5.77.
17. Cmnd. 7306, para. 118.
18. Hansard, 22.11.79.
19. The Scotsman, 24.11.77.
20. Evening Times, 7.2.78.
21. Hansard, 22.11.79.
22. Review of the Operation of the Prevention of Terrorism (Temporary Provisions) Acts 1974 and 1976, Cmnd. 7324, (HMSO 1978).
23. Home Office Statistical Bulletin, 7/80.
24. Sunday Mail, 1.7.79.
25. Cmnd. 2152, (HMSO 1963) para. 230.
26. Hansard, 6.4.78.
27. Hansard, 2.3.78.
28. Calgacus Review No. 2, 1975.
29. The Times, 23/24.9.75.
30. See especially Bunyan, and Ackroyd et al.
31. Cmnd. 7873 (HMSO 1980).
32. 7 Days, 18.11.77.
33. Glasgow News, 26.6.73.
34. 7 Days, 2.12.77.
35. 16.6.78.
36. Quoted in 7 Days, 2.12.77.
37. Quoted in State Research Bulletin No. 3.
38. 9.2.78.
39. The Scotsman, 6.3.78.
40. The Scotsman, 9.3.78., emphasis added.
41. Glasgow Herald, 21.4.79.
42. Sunday Mail, 2.5.79.
43. The Scotsman, 31.10.79.
44. Aliens Restriction (Amendment) Act 1919. This amended legislation first passed in 1905.
45. see, for example, Robin Cook's Security Services Bill (1980) which sought to control the activities of the Special Branch and the Security Service (MI5).

5. Technology and Policing

Since the 1960s the police, at both national and local levels, have adapted technological advancements to their own uses and, in addition, through the work of the Police Scientific Development Branch which was set up in 1963, undertaken original scientific research. In Scotland, this rapid development has stood in marked contrast to the technological backwardness which persisted in many forces until well after the Second World War. The use of computers for the storage and retrieval of information has been the most obvious facet of the new policing technology and the central features of the system nationally are the Police National Computer (PNC), which has now been in operation for five years and which continues to be further developed, and the Metropolitan Police National Intelligence Computer; but increasing use is also being made of computers at a more limited, local level.(1)

In discussing the use of computers by the police it is important to keep in mind the distinction made by the Data Protection Committee in its report (2) between criminal **information** which is hard factual data such as name, date of birth, description, previous convictions etc., and criminal **intelligence** which 'may be speculative, suppositional, hearsay and unverified, such as notes about places frequented, known associates, suspected activities, or even just that a certain car was believed to have been involved in a certain robbery'.(3)

The Police National Computer

Every force in the United Kingdom has direct access to the Police National Computer situated at Hendon in North London which has been operational since 1974. The computers, three

Burroughs 6700s, have the capacity to hold up to 40 million records and the unit is now being equipped with new hardware 'to accommodate the increased volumes of its present and already planned operations'. The Data Protection Committee was told 'that this is entirely due to the natural growth which affects most systems after first estimate, rather than to any major extension of the PNC's work.'(4)

The PNC has five major divisions; the index to national records in the Criminal Records Office; a file of vehicle owners; a file of stolen and suspect vehicles; an index to the national fingerprint collection; and a file of wanted/missing persons.

The criminal names index holds the 3.8 million records held at New Scotland Yard which in turn were based on information supplied by regional forces. There is, however, no index to the records of regional and Scottish criminal records offices. The PNC file shows names, addresses, aliases, dates and place of birth of the subject 'and certain "indicators" (e.g. that the conviction was for an offence involving violence or firearms, pointers to relevant CRO records, or an indication that the Special Branch has an interest in the subject.)'(5) Although the file was supposed to include only the more serious offences recorded at Scotland Yard a considerable number of petty offences, including petty thefts, wasting police time and offences under the Rent Acts, were included during the transfer to the PNC.(6)

The index of vehicle owners has been operational since 1974 and will eventually hold details, including the name and address, of every vehicle keeper in England, Scotland and Wales. The index is updated daily from information supplied by the Driver and Vehicle Licensing Centre in Swansea. This partial duplication of the DVLC's files was explained by the Data Protection Committee on the basis that it 'serves' to enable the police to obtain an immediate response to enquiries about vehicles concerned with crime'.(7) This may well be true but it is equally true that it has other uses. Each record on the file has details of the vehicle, its colour and make, and the name and address of its owner, but it also has space for up to 120 words of descriptive text which could, for example, contain an indicator that there was a Special Branch interest. The file is sub-divided into three categories: (SUS)—temporarily suspected of being used in a crime: (POL)—being used for police purposes; and (INT)—of long term interest to the police: This last category includes those active in some form of public service, e.g. senior police officers, judges and doctors etc. but it may also have others who are of interest to the police for different reasons.

The file of stolen and suspect vehicles also became operational in 1974 and now deals with over 20,000 enquiries per day. According to a 1976 private conference paper quoted in 'New Scientist'(8) 'There are eleven reasons why a vehicle can be recorded in this index, ranging from having been stolen to being owned by an active criminal or having been impounded.' and in fact only 30,000 of the (1976) total of 120,000 records were actually stolen. The remainder include legitimate entries but also, it is now clear, files on 'suspected' vehicles. In a well publicised case in 1977 three members of the Hunt Saboteurs Association were identified after the police had checked their car with the PNC and had been informed that the owner of the car was a prominent member of the Anti-Blood Sports League (sic). The matter was raised in parliament by Jo Richardson M.P. and Dr. Summerskill, replying for the Home Office, denied that political information was stored on the PNC but went on to say: 'Ocasionally information about association with an organisation has been held for a limited period in the index of stolen and suspect vehicles when a police officer has judged it relevant when reporting a vehicle as suspected of being used in connection with a crime.'(9)

The national fingerprint collection holds 2.2 million records and the wanted/missing persons index is expected to cover 50,000 when it is added in the near future. The latter file will not only record names, and the national CRO reference number if the subject has one, but may hold information about known associates, whether the subject is believed to be violent or armed and there will also be a 'free text' space for additional comments which could no doubt include an indication of Special Branch interest.

The PNC is linked to over 800 divisional police offices

throughout the U.K. and can handle 50 messages per second and provide a response within ten seconds. The officer on the beat or in a car can therefore have ready access to the computers' millions of files by means of a radio call to his or her headquarters or divisional office, the whole process probably taking no more than 90 seconds. Officers and civilians in all Scottish forces receive training at Durham in the use of the PNC and there are now over 2 million transactions each year with the computer from Scotland alone; the annual increase in use being of the order of 20%.

National Intelligence Computer

The Metropolitan Police 'C' Department computer is of considerable importance nationally since it holds the records not only of the Metropolitan Police Criminal Intelligence and Fraud Squads but also the records of three national intelligence units—the Central Drugs Intelligence Unit, the Illegal Immigration Unit and the Special Branch. This computer system, brought into operation in the early and mid 1970s, is situated at Tintagel House in London, and is shrouded in official secrecy. In discussing the system in its report, the Data Protection Committee stated '...the observations we make are of value only to the extent that the information on which they are based is adequate; in the case of the Metropolitan Police we have not been able to satisfy ourselves that this is so.'(10) The Committee had therefore to work on the basis of two articles in 'The Times' and some parliamentary answers but further information has come to light since it reported.(11)

According to Duncan Campbell (12) Special Branch files in 1974 (when the operational requirements of the computer system were prepared) numbered 850,000 (including 300,000 containing special, more detailed information) and were estimated by the police to increase at the rate of 1,000 per month to a total of 982,000 by 1985. In the case of the Immigration Intelligence Unit the figure was 13,000 in 1974 growing to 60,000; and in the case of the Drugs Intelligence Unit 76,000 growing to 287,000. While the Special Branch and Immigration Intelligence files do not mention 'crime' or 'criminals' at all, less than two per cent of the Drugs Intelligence files are concerned with those with criminal convictions.

The computer system can provide, in addition, for multifactor searches, that is, as the DPC noted 'it could answer the question: 'Which red-haired Irishman on record drives a white Cortina with MR and 6 in the registration?', and is a Full Text Retrieval system which said the DPC 'introduces a new dimension of unease.'(13) The Committee concluded its discussion of the 'C' Department computer: 'While we have no reason to believe that the public need be unduly alarmed by the general use of computers for police purposes, in relation to the Metropolitan Police we do not have enough evidence to give a firm assurance to that effect for all aspects of such use by them.'(14)

Local Police Computers

In addition to using the Police National Computer and the National Intelligence Computer, several Scottish police forces have their own computers and all make some use of local authority computing facilities. Details of these were given in parliament in 1978 by the Under Secretary of State at the Scottish Home and Health Department.(15) Thus, Strathclyde Police have a Ferranti Argus 500, Argus 700, a Micro computer and a Mini computer; Central and Tayside have Mini computers: and Fife has a CYFAS system. Some of these facilities, whether used solely by the police or shared with the local authority, are used merely for administrative purposes including pay and personnel records, and accident and crime statistics, etc; others have additional functions.

Tayside Police store criminal records on a computer shared with Tayside Regional Council which makes it possible to see criminal records and information about suspects on a visual display unit (VDU) at divisional police offices, and Dumfries and Galloway criminal records were added to this in 1978 as the first step towards a computerised system of national criminal records.

Lothian and Borders Police are proceeding with their own computer project which will provide facilities for crime reporting including multi factor search capabilities, which enable it to identify subjects sharing a number of given characteristics, and would include an index of criminals 'of active interest to the police, their personal details, associates and vehicles used.' The computer system, expected to cost around £1m will be linked directly to the Police National Computer and, when it is established, the Scottish Criminal Records Office computer.(16)

Of the computers used solely by the police the command and control system of Strathclyde Police is believed to be one of the most advanced in the world and attracted visits in 1978 from police representatives from West Germany, Turkey, Saudi Arabia, Iran and the United States.

Command and control systems are designed to collate information of incidents and requests for police assistance with information of the resources which are available, so that a more efficient and faster use of such resources is possible. They were first introduced in Britain in 1972 with a joint Home Office Police Scientific Development Branch/Birmingham City Police experiment.

The Strathclyde system was the second such system and was brought into effect in 1975 at a cost of £835,000. Its annual costs are now around £50,000—£60,000.(17) It deals with around 9,000 incidents each week and was described by the chief constable as being 'invaluable' during the firemen's strike in 1978. Similar facilities are being provided for Tayside Police at a cost of around £80,000.(18) For the country as a whole, a new prototype computer system has been developed (in conjunction with the Department of Physiology at Aberdeen University) for the handling of information about facial features.

It should be clear then that the function of computerisation has not been simply to make policing more efficient by saving time or other resources. Computerisation has provided for qualitative as well as quantitative changes to occur, not only allowing for more and more factual information to be stored than would have been possible previously but, more important, to provide for the linking of unrelated facts. When carried out with factual information such linkage is, at the very least, an intrusion of privacy especially as a piece of information may have been supplied by a subject willingly for a particular purpose and then used without his/her knowledge for a purpose which is completely different. Thus, every vehicle owner knows of the legal obligation to register vehicles with the Driver and Vehicle Licensing Centre at Swansea, but no owner is told, nor does the registration application form state, that the information supplied will automatically be transferred to the Police National Computer. Such transfers occur, despite the Government's assurance in the White Paper 'Computers and Privacy'(19) that 'People asked to provide information should have a right to know for what purposes it will be used, and who is likely to have access to it... information should not be used for a purpose other than one for which it was given or obtained without either the consent of the person whom it concerns, or some authorised justification.' (20) But the danger to the individual becomes more serious when the linkage is between information and intelligence. What is being considered then is not merely an intrusion of privacy but the means for the state and its agencies to keep under surveillance those whose ideas and attitudes are not those of the consensus. At a stage beyond surveillance, the ground is prepared for the harrassment, individually and collectively, of those same people. As Bunyan points out, many of those politically active acquire a criminal record either socially through drugs offences, or on demonstrations, or through everyday harrassment. When this increasing criminalisation is seen together with a widening definition of who is or may be 'subversive', and the growth in numbers and activities of the Special Branch, then the uses of this kind of material, actual or potential, become quite clear.

Firearms and riot equipment

Officers in all Scottish police forces undergo some form of training in the use of firearms although details are difficult to obtain. In Dumfries and Galloway, training is limited to 'selected marksmen'; in Strathclyde the number given training in 1977 was 834, about 13 per cent of the force, including as noted above, all members of the Support Units; in Fife and Grampian the figure is around 6 per cent while in the Northern

Constabulary approximately 33 per cent of serving officers underwent firearms training of some kind—65 on initial courses and 123 on 'refresher' courses, and a number of officers from Scottish forces have received training as 'Public Order' instructors at the Police College at Hendon in North London.

The weapons used are the .38 Smith and Wesson revolver, and, probably, the L39A1 high velocity rifle which is known to be held by other forces and which, according to Bunyan, was 'rejected by the New York police as being too dangerous for use in cities, as its bullets are capable of penetrating several walls and injuring innocent bystanders. The International Red Cross has also condemned it because its bullets have the same effect as dum-dum bullets—the sheer impact can lead to death.'(21)

The change over to this new sophisticated weaponry was made following the report of the working party on the use of firearms in peace time which comprised representatives of the police, army and civil service along with arms experts from the arms manufacturing industry.(22)

But firearms are not the only 'hardware' available to the police. Every force is believed to have a number of riot defence shields(23) and the annual report for 1978 of the chief constable of Dumfries and Galloway stated that: 'Planning for all aspects of serious confrontation situations necessitated the purchase of shields and other equipment and the continuation of specialised training.' If the smallest force in Scotland holds such equipment it is reasonable to assume that this is true of other forces also and such an assumption is backed up by recent press reports of riot training. The 'Sunday Mail' reported in February 1979 that police officers were receiving secret training in the use of riot shields, helmets and other anti-riot weapons and that the training, at the Scottish Police College, had been started after demands by the Scottish Police Federation. The Federation's Secretary was quoted as saying: 'We feel that Scottish policemen are not trained properly. It is only a question of time before the violence in London occurs here.' All the police forces, except Grampian and Tayside, both of which refused to comment, said that they had instituted an anti-riot training programme.(24) A further report in an Edinburgh magazine stated that Lothian and Borders police were receiving riot training at Redford Barracks, Edinburgh, in preparation for the occupation in June 1979 of the proposed site for the advanced gas cooled reactor at Torness. Lothian and Borders police 'definitely would not comment' on the reports and in the event relied on the non-violence and self-policing of the demonstrators.(25)

The police in Scotland have yet to appear in public with anti-riot equipment and recent public order tactics have remained in the tradition of containment by force of numbers. Thus when a National Front election meeting took place in Glasgow in May 1979, 1,000 officers were on duty to face 500 peaceful anti-fascist demonstrators. The force included 40 dogs, 20 mounted police and 'Special Branch officers with cine cameras picking out ringleaders' (of the anti-fascists).(26)

In 1980, on two occasions, a similar police presence was augmented by a police helicopter hired from the Metropolitan Police.

NOTES

1. This section only attempts a sketch of the police use of computers. For a fuller account see Duncan Campbell: 'Society Under Surveillance' in Hain (ed).
2. Report of the Committee on Data Protection (DPC), Cmnd. 7341 (HMSO 1978).
3. ibid, para. 8.05.
4. ibid, para. 8.17.
5. ibid, para. 8.08.
6. New Scientist, 18.1.79.
7. DPC 8.09.
8. 18.1.79.

9. Hansard, 2.12.79.
10. DPC 8.03.
11. see Campbell, op. cit.
12. ibid.
13. DPC 8.22.
14. ibid, para. 8.23.
15. Hansard, 16.11.78.
16. State Research Bulletin No. 16.
17. Hansard, 2.2.79.
18. ibid.
19. Cmnd. 6353 (HMSO 1975).
20. ibid, para. 34.
21. Bunyan, p. 93.
22. ibid.
23. Glasgow Herald, 22.8.77.
24. Sunday Mail, 18.2.79.
25. City Lynx, 4.5.79.
26. Sunday Mail, 2.5.79.

6. Control of the Police

Police Authorities

Police forces in Scotland have always been under local, as opposed to central government, control. (The development of this local control is dealt with in more detail in Part One.) There has traditionally been a hostility towards the idea of a centralised national police force, subject to direction and control by central government. The idea of local control of the police continues today in the form of local police authorities and the theory remains that the accountability, such as it is, of the police to the community is to be found in the relationship of the police force and its chief constable to the police authority, rather than in any relationship between chief constables and central government departments.

For the greater part of the twentieth century the system of local control of the police has been significantly different in Scotland from that in England and Wales. A modern police authority in Scotland does not include anyone who is not an elected councillor, whereas in England it is made up of two thirds councillors plus one third local magistrates. In practice, however, the difference is difficult to discern.

Reviewing the position in 1962 the Royal Commission on the Police was unhappy about the composition of Scottish police authorities. It noted that in theory, while the official authority was the full council, in practice it found that, as happens with other local authority functions such as housing or social work, police business was dealt with in the first instance by a police committee. Its decisions were then subject to ratification by the full council. 'The police committee has no powers of its own, nor has it any legal standing' said the Commission.(1)

In the case of joint police forces the functions of the police authority were carried out by an ad hoc body, usually composed of representatives of the constituent authorities, each of which retained the title of police authority even though they had 'no police and little authority over a combined force'.(2)

The Commission went on to accept that magistrates were of less importance in Scotland than in England and should therefore continue to be excluded from police authorities (unless, of course, as frequently happened, they were also local councillors). It continued: 'We do not, however, regard the whole council as a suitable body to discuss and finally decide the important matters which arise in connection with the police. We accordingly recommend that statutory provision be made for the appointment of a committee of the local authority to be the police authority.'(3)

For combined forces the Commission recommended that the joint police committee be given the title of police authority and that local councils both lose the title and their largely theoretical right to challenge estimates of the joint committee.

The Royal Commission's recommendation was never made into law, but its intention has to some extent been achieved indirectly by the development of local government. Although the police committee continues to have no powers of its own nor any legal standing and while committee decisions still require the ratification of the full council, (except in the case of joint forces) the re-organisation and centralisation of local government has given even greater real powers to the committees and to the relevant non-elected officials than was previously the case.

A clear example of this process came in 1978 when the Police and Fire Committee of Strathclyde Regional Council authorised an 'out of court' settlement of £2,000 to be made to a man suing the police for injuries received while in custody. The relevant minute of the committee reads: 'After consideration and having heard the Depute Director of Administration regarding the case of McCulloch v the Chief Constable, the committee homologated the action taken by the chairman in authorising the Director of Administration to deal with the matter on the lines indicated.'(4) This minute was formally ratified without discussion—along with the minutes of several other committees—at the next neeting of the full council the following month. Yet several councillors claimed that the first they learned of the settlement was when it was announced in court on 10th October. This case indicates a general weakness in police authority practice. The decision to make the payment was in effect taken by senior non-elected officials along with the committee chairman, ratified by a committee which seemed not to be fully aware of what it was agreeing to—one member of the committee, Councillor John Fitch told the 'Glasgow Herald': 'If this decision was minuted then it must have been meaningless to us when it was presented and slipped through without discussion. We rubber stamp a lot of minutes put before us by officials and sometimes the words used are vague and we just agree without discussion.'(5) That decision was in turn ratified without discussion by the full Regional Council.

But this weakness of practice is underpinned by the weakness of the police authority's statutory functions and by the way in which these have been restrictively interpreted, both by committee members and by the courts. The police authority's general responsibilities are the payment of police officers, the provision of buildings and equipment and the fixing of the local force strength. Scottish police authorities have no express statutory duty 'to secure the maintenance of an adequate and efficient police force for the area' which is imposed on English police authorities(6) although this is implied in their other specified functions. With the approval of the Secretary of State it appoints the chief constable and it may, again with the Secretary of State's approval, require the chief constable to resign 'in the interests of efficiency'. But it has a very limited role in controlling what the police actually do and how their strength is deployed. It receives the chief constable's annual report on policing and crime and has power to request further reports on 'matters connected with the policing of the area for which the force is maintained.'(7) But the scope of this is limited since 'information which in the public interest ought not to be disclosed, or is not needed for the discharge of the function of the police authority' need not be included unless the Secretary of State confirms the police authority's right to require it.(8) Similarly the police authority has a duty to keep itself informed about the manner in which complaints against police officers are dealt with, but it has no power to instruct a chief constable to direct his officers in a certain way or to influence directly the policing of an area. There is, in fact, no evidence that police authorities in Scotland have attempted to control policing in this way.

Even the power to request reports from the chief constable and presumably thereby at the very least to initiate a discussion is little used, if at all. Thus, for example, on two occasions when a particular aspect of police operations in Strathclyde has been publicly and extensively criticised, the Police and Fire Committee has not even discussed the matter. The first case was that of a National Front meeting in Glasgow in June 1975 when over 100 anti-fascist demonstrators were arrested. Criticism centred on the force used by the police, especially by the Support Units. (See page 46). The second occasion was that of the attempted bribery by a Special Branch officer of a student at Paisley College of Technology to spy on his fellow students. The then convenor of the Police and Fire Committee, Mrs. Agnes Ballantyne told 'The Scotsman' that 'she had no plans to raise the issue with the Chief Constable. If there had been an increase in Special Branch activity she was sure it was justified.'(9)

So, even on a brief examination of the work of police authorities (or more realistically, of the police committees) it is difficult to avoid the conclusion that the police authority is little more than a paymaster for the force, providing the necessary finance and physical facilities, but having little control over how such resources are used. Their powers and functions may be limited and subject to control by the Secretary of State but even when they have been presented with an opportunity to assert some measure of control over a disturbing practice the police authorities appear singularly to have failed.

Central Government

The Secretary of State for Scotland has a number of important administrative functions covering the police—but he is not a police authority in the sense just discussed. It is through the Secretary of State that the 50 per cent revenue grant is made to police authorities. He is responsible for ratifying a number of decisions made by the police authorities, such as the appointment of chief constables(10) or the fixing of the force establishment. He makes regulations covering the government and administration of police forces including the qualifications for appointment and promotion, the maintenance of discipline, the wages and conditions of service, duties to be performed. These are distributed to chief constables in regular circulars from the Department's Edinburgh headquarters. The Scottish Secretary is also responsible for training facilities and courses and acts as an appellate body for officers dealt with for disciplinary offences. In parliament the Secretary of State frequently provides general factual and statistical information about the police, strengths, complaints, etc. and will on occasion answer questions on matters for which he is not strictly speaking responsible. But questions relating to police operations are invariably ruled out of order.

Most of the Secretary of State's functions relevant to the police are carried out by the Scottish Home and Health Department, a sub-division of the Scottish Office. An Under-Secretary of State has particular governmental responsibility. The department is divided into specific divisions; those concerned with policing are:

IB : Police services
IC : Fire services; home defence; emergency services co-ordination
IIA : Law and general
IIB : Prisons
IIC : Criminal justice and licensing.

Two under-secretaries have responsibilities for divisions IB and IC, and for IIA, B and C respectively and each division is itself headed by an assistant secretary.

The Secretary of State has, in addition, the same power as

the police authority to request reports from a chief constable on 'matters connected with the policing of an area for which the force is maintained'.(11) As in the case of police authorities, however, this power is rarely, if ever, exercised. Things might have been different, though. In 1953 the Scottish Local Government Law Consolidation Committee recommended that the Secretary of State should be entitled to give instructions to chief constables 'in any case' and a clause to this effect was included in the Committee's draft bill. The provision would have given the Secretary of State considerable powers of direct control, buth it was withdrawn after protest from local authorities and others before being presented to parliament.(12)

However, the law does give the Secretary of State the power to hold a local enquiry into 'any matter connected with the policing of an area.'(13)

This power might in theory allow a degree of direct central control over police operations but it has never been used. In 1959 though, a Tribunal of Inquiry was set up under previous legislation to investigate an allegation that two police officers in Thurso (Caithness) had assaulted a fifteen year old boy, John Waters. The affair was one of the events leading to the setting up of the Royal Commission on the Police in 1960 and was surprising not because it was set up at all but because the allegation—of a single blow found by the tribunal to have taken place—was quite trivial by comparison with what was alleged elsewhere at the same time and has been alleged with equal weight since.(14)

The Secretary of State is also responsible for the direction of the work of the Inspectorate of Constabulary, first established in 1857. Until the Second World War the Inspector was usually a retired armed services officer but is now invariably a former senior police officer. The modern duties of the Inspectorate of Constabulary are 'to visit and inquire into the state and efficiency of the police forces and of the buildings and equipment used by such forces', and to submit to the Secretary of State an annual report on the state and efficiency of police forces. This report is laid before parliament and is published. In carrying out their work the inspectors visit each force at least once a year but retain regular contact with senior police officers for example through their attendance at meetings of the Association of Chief Police Officers (Scotland). The inspectorate is also represented on the board of governors of the Scottish Police College and provides a link with such bodies as the Police Scientific Development Branch which is concerned with the adaptation of technological advances to policing.

The theory of control of the police is therefore based on two myths. First, there is the myth that the police are accountable at a local level to the elected representatives of those whom they are employed to police. Not only are the powers of the police authorites limited in law but they have failed to assert themselves when an opportunity arises. Second, there is the myth that the police are free from central control other than on administrative matters. The circulars from the Scottish Home and Health Department, the Department's provision of training and research facilities, the direction of the Inspectorate of Constabulary and the inspector's continuing contact and influence with the chief constables and central administration all belie the notion of relatively independent and autonomous police forces free from central political control.

NOTES

1. Cmnd. 1728 (HMSO 1962) para. 213.
2. ibid, para. 215.
3. ibid, para. 217.
4. Strathclyde Regional Council minutes, October 1978, p. 1143.
5. 11.10.78.
6. Police Act 1964, s.4.
7. Police (Scotland) Act, 1967, s.15. (For an examination of Scottish chief constables' Annual Reports see State Research Bulletin No. 12.
8. ibid.
9. 9.2.78.
10. See the case of Magistrates of Kilmarnock v. Secretary of State for Scotland, (1961 Scots Law Times, 333.)
11. s. 15 1967 Act.
12. Cmnd. 8993, (HMSO 1953) para. 10.
13. s. 29, 1967 Act.
14. See Report of the Tribunal appointed to inquire into the allegation of assault on John Waters, Cmnd. 718 (HMSO 1959).

7. Complaints Against the Police

The Police Act 1976 which set up the Police Complaints Board for England and Wales and created a limited system of review of police complaints, does not apply to Scotland and complaints against the police continue to be investigated by the police themselves. A complainer has no possibility of a formal appeal against, or review of, a finding, although a police officer has the usual rights of appeal if found guilty in a court of law and if found guilty of a police disciplinary offence he can appeal to the Secretary of State.

The investigation of complaints is the responsibility of the force deputy chief constable who must first of all decide whether there is any suggestion of a criminal offence in the complaint. If there is he will make enquiries and submit a report to the procurator fiscal who will in turn order further enquiries to be made by the police and may interview witnesses before reporting to the Crown Office for further instructions.

The actual investigation of the complaint is carried out by an investigating officer of the rank of inspector or above, appointed by the deputy chief constable. After interviewing the complainer and any other witnesses (although not the officer complained of) he submits a report on the basis of which the deputy chief constable decides whether or not the officer is to be charged with an offence against the Discipline Code which is part of the Police Regulations.(1) The code specifies a number of offences including incivility, drinking on duty, taking bribes, using unnecessary force, suppression or falsification of complaints, and conviction of a criminal offence. The hearing of a disciplinary offence is conducted by the chief constable (not the deputy) and a finding of guilt can result in dismissal from the force, being required to resign, reduction in rank, reduction in rate of pay, a fine, reprimand or caution. If only a minor breach of the Discipline Code has occurred the officer may simply be warned without proceeding to a hearing. As noted above a police officer found guilty of a disciplinary offence may appeal to the Secretary of State.

The deputy chief constable may of course also decide that the complaint is not substantiated in which case the complainer is simply informed by a brief letter which sets out no evidence for such a decision.

In recent years the number of formal complaints lodged has remained relatively stable. In 1978, 1,183 complaints were made; of these 345 (approximately one third) were either withdrawn or not proceeded with by the complainer; 32 were resolved by an explanation to the complainer and 596 were rejected as unsubstantiated. 499 were reported to the procurator fiscal for consideration of criminal proceedings but in only 7 cases did prosecution actually occur. It is impossible to go beyond these figures and the picture they provide is a very partial one. The experience of the Scottish Council for Civil Liberties and many practising solicitors is that while many complaints may be quite trivial, large numbers of people do not even bother to make a formal complaint because they have no confidence that their complaint will be investigated impartially—even where it is likely that the procurator fiscal will be involved—that their chances of success are slim, that they lack independent witnesses, or because they fear harrassment by the police if they do pursue a complaint.

Occasionally, the problem is highlighted. In 1974, for example, a Glasgow councillor, Bill Hattan, compiled a dossier of cases which he described as 'a challenge to the conscience of the Labour Movement'. Hattan had been contacted by a number of parents in his ward and questioned both them and their sons about their allegations. He published a 24 page report of complaints and noted: 'I am satisfied there is substance in the allegations, and that there is indeed cause for great concern at what is happening in our city.' His introduction to the report concluded: 'I believe Chief Constables have got to be told to root out the elements responsible for the kind of thing which is happening, and the Labour movement should launch a national campaign to secure the appointment of Independent Commissioners who will receive, hear, investigate and report on complaints against the Police.'

Hattan's report received considerable publicity both locally and nationally and his local constituency Labour Party presented a motion to the annual conference of the Scottish Council of the Labour Party in March 1974. In proposing the motion he said this publicity 'has led to my receiving letters from all over the country and has convinced me that the problem of police harrassment is not merely a Scottish one, but in point of fact is a national disgrace. Glasgow M.P.s have told me they could have produced the kind of report I produced. I have been assured of the support of many court lawyers and magistrates. Ministers of religion have gone out of their way to express their agreement with what I have been attempting to do.' The motion, which was carried by conference, called for a statutory Independent Authority for investigating complaints against the police.

At the same time an official report on 'The Handling of Complaints Against the Police' was published.(2) This was the report of a working group set up in 1973 following an attempt by Philip Whitehead M.P. to reform the complaints procedures. (A similar working group was established for England and Wales.) It was in general opposed to any change but recognised that the government had indicated that it was disposed to introduce a limited **ex post facto** review. It sought therefore to influence the form that such a review might take. It recommended a single review body for Scotland, composed of a government appointed chairman 'being a layman of high public reputation'(3), assisted by two advisors, one with experience in police matters, the other legally qualified. The review body would have power to examine: '(a) the procedures adopted by the Chief Constable, his Deputy and the investigating officer; (b) the correctness of these procedures and their conformity with police practice; and (c) the thoroughness and impartiality of the investigation.'(4) The review body was also to be able to examine the deputy chief constable's decisions in referring or not referring a complaint to the procurator fiscal or in instituting or not instituting disciplinary proceedings. It was to be excluded, however, from any consideration of cases reported to the prosecuting authorities, (unless an offence against discipline was involved) and, most important, was not to be able to comment on the outcome of disciplinary proceedings or on any appeal. In short, 'the review body will not review or comment on the conduct which was the subject of the complaint'.(5)

The report of the English working group led to the passing of the Police Act 1976 but it was not until November 1976 that the Labour government introduced the Police (Scotland) Bill.(7) This would have set up a Police Complaints Panel for Scotland, composed of three members appointed by the Secretary of State. The Panel would have been able, at the request of a complainer, to review a decision by the deputy chief constable not to bring disciplinary charges against a police officer, and would have had powers to recommend and, in the last resort, instruct the bringing of such charges. It would have had no powers in respect of matters referred to the procurator fiscal for the consideration of criminal proceedings. The function of the Panel was therefore extremely limited—even more so than that recommended by the working party. The Bill was not, however, to proceed very far.

Bruce Millan, then Secretary of State, did not seek a second reading for the Bill despite the collapse of the devolution bill which left a large gap in Scottish parliamentary business. 'The Scotsman' newspaper was left to draw the obvious conclusion. 'Controversial proposals for a new complaints procedure for the police in Scotland have been put on ice by the Government because of the continuing dispute over the police pay claim. Ministers are holding back the Police (Scotland) Bill because they fear it would exacerbate relations with the police, who are furious with the government for refusing their claim for a £6 a week pay rise ..... but Ministers insist that there is no question of the Government dropping the measure, and that it will be put through Parliament as soon as the pay claim is settled and relations with the police improve.'(8) Pay, however, was not the only issue. The government was keenly aware of the opposition expressed to similar reforms in England and Wales and only two months previously the Deputy Chief Constable of Strathclyde Police, Elphinstone Dalglish, had told the Police and Fire Committee that reforms could lead to 'an undermining of the Chief Constable's authority in the eyes of rank and file members of the force.' Mr. Dalglish also told the committee that police representatives had had meetings with senior civil servants to discuss the bill. 'Their point of view had been listened to because the civil servants had recognised that Strathclyde Police represented half the police officers in Scotland and if the system did not work there then it would not work anywhere.'(9) It was not necessary, however, for such veiled warnings to be developed or for senior officers to follow the example of Metropolitan Police Commissioner Robert Mark who made it known that his early retirement was in protest at the reforms. At the end of the year it was reported that 'The Government have shelved for the second time controversial proposals to reform the procedure for making complaints against the police in Scotland'(10), and this was despite the interim settlement of the police pay dispute. The last had been heard of the Police (Scotland) Bill. The Conservative Manifesto for Scotland 1979 stated: 'We envisage no change in police disciplinary procedures.'

In addition to being subject to the criminal law the police are also open in theory to actions for damages in the civil courts but cases are extremely rare. Although chief constables are now liable for the actions of their officers and the police authority is liable for any damages which might be awarded (or any settlement out of court) (11), a person whishing to sue the police not only faces difficulties of evidence but must also aver and prove malice and want of reasonable cause on the part of the police officer. The difficulties in proving unlawful arrest are well illustrated by the case of Mr. Swankie in 1973.(12) Swankie was stopped by plain clothes police while driving his car. His keys were taken from him and the police waited with him at the car until uniformed officers arrived to carry out a breath test. Part of Swankie's appeal against a conviction for drunken driving was the legality of the arrest by the plain clothes officers but the Appeal Court held that

Swankie had not been unlawfully arrested—he had not been arrested at all but detained—a concept unknown to Scots law. Successful civil actions on other grounds are also rare. One such case was resolved in 1978 with an out of court settlement, believed to amount to £2,000 paid by Strathclyde Regional Council on behalf of the chief constable, to a man who alleged that, four years previously, his jaw had been broken by police officers after he stuck his tongue out at them.(13)

NOTES

1. Police (Discipline) (Scotland) Regulations 1967 (1967 No. 1021 [S80]).
2. Cmnd. 5583. (HMSO 1974).
3. ibid, para. 41.
4. ibid, para. 26.
5. ibid, para. 30.
6. for the background to the development of the new complaints system see State Research Bulletin No. 1 and 6.
7. Bill 9, Session 1976-77.
8. 29.3.77.
9. The Scotsman, 26.1.77.
10. The Scotsman, 27.12.77.
11. Police (Scotland) Act, 1967. s.39.
12. Swankie v Milne (1973 SLT [Notes] 28).
13. Glasgow Herald, The Scotsman, 11.10.78. See also pp. 78-9

8. Politics and Policing

One of the most significant developments in post war policing in the United Kingdom has been the increasing reluctance of the police, most notably chief police officers, to remain within the boundaries of their traditional role as enforcers of the law and they have sought increasingly and with no little success to have a direct influence on the content of that law, by telling both the courts how to administer the law and parliament what the law should be. In this way have they openly entered the arena of politics to which previously they had only rarely been permitted access. This expressly political activity has gone beyond the submission of evidence and opinion to Royal Commissions or official committees concerned with law reform which the police and police organisations have traditionally undertaken; it has extended to a more general expression in the media and elsewhere of explicitly political views on crime, social conditions and industrial relations. The lectures and public statements of the former Metropolitan Commissioner, Sir Robert Mark, are the most obvious example of this kind of activity and probably more than any other single person, Mark is responsible for the development, but he has been emulated not only by his successor, Sir David McNee, but also by chief constables of provincial forces including James Anderton, Chief Constable of Greater Manchester, and from a quite different point of view, John Alderson, Chief Constable of Devon and Cornwall.(1)

What is surprising is that this development appears not to have spread to Scotland where none of the chief constables can be said to be anything of a public figure, even on a local or Scottish level. Their names are probably unknown to the vast majority of the public and they appear to eschew publicity even when a platform is offered. This is not because the role of the Scottish police chief is any less important than that of any other.(2) As was noted above, the chief constable of Strathclyde not only commands the largest police force outside the London Metropolitan area but has responsibility for policing over half of Scotland's population, and other chief constables in Scotland have their own special responsibilities, most notably the chief constable of Grampian Police who now has the policing of the North Sea Oil Developments as part of his duties.

There would appear to be two possible reasons for this relative silence.

Firstly, the different legal system in Scotland and the fundamentally different role of the Scottish police in the criminal process have deprived them of many of the grounds of complaint of their English colleagues. That they neither initiate nor conduct prosecutions, and therefore have no direct interest in the prosecution system and the role of the public prosecutor, means that the rate of conviction/acquittal is no reflection on their actions or procedures. In addition, the different use of the jury in Scotland and the absence of a right of an accused to opt for jury trial means that jury trials occur far less frequently than in England and there have been, therefore, no grounds for a similar attack on the jury system to that led in England by Sir Robert Mark.

Secondly, the police in Scotland have not had to deal with political opposition which has, in different forms, faced the English police. At the level of local government as we have seen, the police authorites do not appear to have attempted to intervene in the question of police operations, have remained firmly within their allotted role and have avoided possible confrontation. At the level of central government, changes in the law which have so aroused the anger of English police chiefs, such as the Bail and Police Acts of 1976, did not apply to Scotland and similar changes to which Scottish police chiefs might be opposed have not been proposed. The one attempt, that of the Police (Scotland) Bill 1976 which would have introduced a limited reform of the police complaints procedure, was feebly handled and quickly withdrawn by the government in the fact of opposition.(3) In addition, political opposition to the police on matters of law and law reform has traditionally been weak and the pressure groups so vigorous in England have been absent in Scotland.

What little debate there is in Scotland on policing and related matters takes place therefore within limits far more restrictively defined than in the rest of Britain. A look at the major recent committees on Scots law and procedure reveals not only the highly conservative membership of such bodies (including, invariably, at least one chief constable or assistant chief constable,) but also the establishment bias of the organisations and individuals submitting evidence, including, with some consistency, the three police representative organisations—the Association of Chief Police Officers (Scotland), the Superintendents Association and the Scottish Police Federation. There is, furthermore, the cohesion which exists not only among the senior police officers but almost invariably among the elite groups and senior decision makers in small countries and political systems, as here between police chiefs, politicians and senior administrators.

At yet another level, crime and consequently policing have not taken on the explicitly political dimensions which they have assumed elsewhere in Britain. The colour/racial factors are largely absent, the extreme right has failed even to gain an organisational foothold, industrial action is at most a few scuffles and minor assaults, and Scotland has not had its Notting Hill, Lewisham or Grunwick. It is not surprising then that the traditional platform of the chief constable's annual report to the police authority is limited to commenting upon the state of crime, recruitment to the force and the wages and conditions of police officers, and generally ignores the broader political and social questions of the day. For example, in his report for 1978, the chief constable of Dumfries and Galloway had nothing to say about his Special Branch nor about the fact that the number of detentions under the Prevention of Terrorism Act in the force area was the third highest in the whole of Britain. He did however state that he was 'concerned by the significant increase in the theft and non-recovery of bicycles.'(4)

There are however exceptions to this general rule. The chief constable of Lothian and Borders for example stated in his annual report for 1978 '... and there is concern that inflation, recession and greater unemployment may lead to more labour disputes and demonstrations and consequently a further drain on the manpower available to undertake our primary functions to guard, watch and patrol.' And he commented on the increased number of assaults on the police: 'It may be that the constable in uniform is becoming the scapegoat for those frustrated with society and all its problems.'

While chief constables in Scotland may have been relatively silent on the broader political questions of the day the police as a body or bodies have not. The Scottish Police Federation which represents all ranks up to that of inspector took part in the national 'law and order' campaign run by the Police Federation in the mid-1970s, producing its own leaflet entitled 'Do you want law and order?' This not only called for increased powers for the police but also attacked the way in which young offenders were treated by the criminal law and the parole system. In 1979 the Scottish Federation was also a party to the notorious Police Federation advertisement 'Law and Order' which appeared in almost every national newspaper only two weeks before the general election and which outlined the Federations' demands, including tougher penalties, secure accommodation for young offenders and increased spending on the police.

One week later at the annual conference the Scottish Federation chairman called for an immediate referendum by the new government on the question of capital punishment and attacked 'identifiable people' who were determined to destroy the fabric of society.(5) The following year a similar attack was mounted on those said to be conducting a 'scurrilous campaign... which suggests that some form of legalised murder is regularly perpetrated in police stations throughout the United Kingdom.'(6) As in 1979, these people were not identified nor was any evidence produced to show that those, such as the Scottish Council for Civil Liberties, who had expressed concern at the number of deaths in police custody, had ever suggested, far less used the words, 'legalised murder'.

But the police have also expressed themselves through the medium of the annual report of the Inspectorate of Constabulary, a platform used increasingly in recent years and one more important for the media coverage it inevitably receives than for what it actually says. In the report for 1977 the inspector reported the complaints of officers attending court as witnesses about late changes of pleas and 'spurious pleas of not guilty at the initial pleading diet.'(7), and repeated the complaints of Glasgow detectives at the publication by the Scottish Consumer Council of a booklet outlining the rights of persons when searched or arrested. 'The police feel that too much attention is paid to those who stir up complaints against the police or otherwise make the police job more difficult.'(8) The same report also bemoaned the absence of any right to stop and search people suspected of carrying offensive weapons.

The following year the Inspector of Constabulary continued the attack on legal aid and lawyers saying at the press conference to present his annual report that 'There is an impression that some lawyers are getting their clients to plead not guilty when they know they are guilty. You just have to see the number of lawyers who now have large cars and large houses, who were penniless a few years ago.'(9)

The police in Scotland have not therefore kept out of politics in the way that they once did and in this have followed a national trend, albeit to a lesser extent than the police in England. As far as the chief constables are concerned their relative silence is not due to any fundamental difference between their role and that of chief constables in England. Police chiefs in Scotland have so far been able to pursue their aims through traditional channels and have done so with some success; they successfully helped defeat the proposals to reform the complaints procedure and (at the time of writing) they appear to have been successful in their demands for increased powers. Whether they will continue to adhere to these means or whether, like police chiefs elsewhere, they will develop a new explicitly political role, will depend very much on whether the traditional means continue to be sufficient to their purpose and, of course, on the general political drift in the country.

NOTES

1. For the development of political police chiefs see Martin Kettle: 'The Politics of Policing and the Policing of Politics' in Hain, (ed.).
2. Nor has it anything to do with Scottish laconicism. Sir David McNee, after all, is a Scot who, until his appointment as Metropolitan Commissioner, had served all his police experience in Scotland: so too is James Jardine, Chairman of the Police Federation (of England and Wales). Neither can be described as reticent.
3. see pp. 87-8
4. Annual Report for 1978, p. 6.
5. The Scotsman, 26.4.79.
6. Evening Times, 30.4.80.
7. Cmnd. 7306 (HMSO 1978) p. 33.
8. ibid, p. 35.
9. The Scotsman, 1.11.79.

PART THREE

EMERGENCY PLANNING

Introduction

Twentieth century policing in its broadest sense, that is the maintenance of a given social order or system of control, has since the beginning of this century embraced comprehensive plans for dealing with emergencies or contingencies. Such plans rely not only on the civil police but also on the military and the various parts of the civil administration. An examination of this aspect of policing is an integral part of any study of the contemporary police. The history of state planning for emergencies and contingencies has been well covered elsewhere(1) and it is not intended to cover it here, but a summary is important and may show how the concern of emergency planning has changed over the years.

Before the first world war emergency planning was primarily based on the supposition of attack or invasion by a foreign power but after the conclusion of the war in 1919 the external threat was replaced in government minds by an internal threat from the organised working class. Such an internal threat had always existed as far as the ruling class was concerned (it was not for nothing that the working class was referred to as the 'dangerous classes' in the eighteenth and nineteenth centuries) but the post war years showed just how real a challenge the working class could pose. The Russian revolution, the uprisings in central and eastern Europe were indications abroad; the soldiers and sailors councils, the forty hours movement on Clydeside, and the General Strike of 1926 were indications at home. And it was largely as a result of the events of the 'Red Clydeside' that state emergency planning began to develop.

The collapse of such working class initiatives and movements, the economic crisis of the 1920s and 30s and the ensuing demoralisation of the working class temporarily obliterated any internal challenge to the status quo and the state's main concern became again an external, foreign power and continued to be so through the second world war, the 1950s and into the 1960s. During the Cold War period of the 50s and 60s government expenditure on civil defence increased, including the building of twelve regional seats of government (RSGs) (at an estimated cost of £1.4m)—underground shelters for selected senior personnel from local and central government, the military and the police. The locations of these RSGs, indeed their very existence, was kept secret from the general public until exposed by the Spies for Peace in 1963.(2)

By 1965 however military theorists had largely ruled out any possibility of nuclear attack and deliberate agression in Europe on the basis of mutual deterrence—'detente of the 1970s had clearly been perceived by the government and the state, if not by the public'(3)—and this was officially accepted by the Labour Government's White Paper on defence published in 1965. Three years later, coinciding with rigorous cuts in government expenditure it was announced that Civil Defence, which had been reorganised during the 1950s, was to be placed on a 'care and maintenance' basis. The Civil Defence Corps, numbering 187,000 volunteers, the Auxiliary Force Corps, and large sections of the Territorial Army, were disbanded.

In the 1970s, however, after the Tory government had declared four separate 'states of emergency' between July 1970 and August 1972 in response to industrial action, two separate but connected initiatives were taken in state emergency planning. The first was a reorganisation of civil defence, now to be known as Home Defence, and the second was the redrawing by the military of the National Security or War Plan on the basis of an internal enemy. These two initiatives remain at the core of emergency planning today.

In 1970, the then Prime Minister Edward Heath told the General Assembly of the United Nations that 'We have seen in the last few years the growth of the cult of political violence, preached and practiced not so much between states as within them. It is a sombre thought, but it may that in the 1970s, the decade which faces us, civil war, rather than between nations, will be the main danger we face.' Five years later, Air Marshal, Sir Leslie Mavor, principal of the Home Defence College at Easingwold said 'The full possibility of the present internal threat is only just sinking in.'(4) Official literature and pronouncements on home defence and emergency planning repeatedly refer to the similarities between war and 'major peacetime emergencies' and the two have become almost synonymous.

Events in the middle east, especially in Iran, and in Afghanistan in 1979 led to increased scares of the possibility of nuclear war and an increased general interest in Britain's home defence preparations and at the end of 1979 it was announced by the government that there was to be an internal Home Office review of home defence. This review, the findings of which had not yet been announced at the time of going to press, was probably the most important such review ever and certainly indicated the biggest upheaval in home defence since the revival of the system under Heath in the early 1970s. It would be quite wrong however to see in this renewed interest and official review any change of heart on the part of the British government or military.

The review springs from no humanitarian concern for the British public; the idea of saving any substantial number of the public from the effects of nuclear attack was abandoned long ago and is not now being disinterred. Despite the events in Afghanistan and Iran and the revival of the Cold War the British state is still as much concerned with internal defence as it is with defence against external attack and even if this were not true it still has no intention of spending any resources on protection for the general public. As before it is concerned to protect only a small elite—politicians, military personnel, administrators—and indeed the occasion of the review will doubtless provide the opportunity for the state to complete its building programme and other preparations for the protection of such people. In addition, the increasing polarisation in British society and especially the coming to power of a government bent on policies of confrontation means that the internal threat is seen as more important, not less so.

The reader may well disagree with this view but it must be emphasised that the preparations described in this section, whether described as home defence, civil defence or more generally as emergency planning, although they may be used in ways which genuinely benefit the public and not just an elite section of it, have in the past been used against the public and can be so used again.

1. Home Defence and Internal Defence

The Regional Government System

In the event of a prolonged national emergency, for example a general strike, insurrection or major natural disaster, the administration of Britain would pass to a system of Regional Government. There are twelve regional government areas (known in official parlance as Home Defence Regions) in the country, of which Scotland is one—Region 11. Scotland is further divided into three zones (equivalent to sub-regions in England), Western, Eastern and Northern, which are themselves divided into areas. This division of the country was adjusted in 1975 at the same time as the reorganisation of local government and the police and the regions now largely coincide with the ten Army UK Land Forces (UKLF) Districts and to the regional areas of the Territorial Army, the regular army's volunteer reserve force.

The Western Zone of Region 11 includes most of Strathclyde and all of Dumfries and Galloway; the Eastern Zone comprises Lothian and Borders; and the Northern Zone includes Central Region, Tayside, Fife, the Highlands and Islands, Grampian and the north of Strathclyde.

In political and administrative command of the Region would be a Regional Commissioner who has already been designated and who would probably be a local politician of ministerial rank, most probably the Secretary of State for Scotland, or possibly one of the junior ministers at the Scottish Office. (During the General Strike of 1926 the Commissioner was the Lord Advocate, William Watson, while during the Second World War the post was held by Thomas Johnston, a former Scottish under Secretary, succeeded by Lord Rose-berry, Lord Lieutenant of Midlothian, later to become Secret-ary of State for Scotland.)

The Regional Commissioner would be one of a triumvirate consisting of the Regional Military Commander, presumably the General Officer Commanding (GOC) HQ Scotland (pres-ently Lieutenant General Sir Michael Gow), and the Regional Police Commander, the Chief Inspector of Constabulary (Edward Frizzell). Similar appointments would exist at zone and area level and various individuals have already been designated to such posts.

Both the Regional Commissioner and Zone Commissioners (and their supporting staffs) would operate from purpose built shelters each of which provides accommodation, supplies, communications equipment including telephone lines, tele-printers, radio equipment and broadcasting studios. The Northern Zone Control is situated in Anstruther near Dundee, the Eastern Zone Control at the army camp at Kirknewton near Edinburgh, and the Western Zone Control probably at Prestwick on the Ayrshire coast.(5)

The site of the central Regional Control for Scotland is not known but it is situated in one of the Armed Forces Head-quarters (AFHQ) which replaced Regional Seats of Govern-ment in the mid-1970s. It has been suggested that AFHQ for Scotland is in fact also at Kirknewton along with the East-ern Zone Control.(6)

Communications

In any emergency, communications systems are of primary importance and the state has made this area one of top priority in its planning. According to Laurie the various parts of the emergency system are linked by specially 'hardened' tele-phone lines, following existing trunk cable routes. While this safeguards communications between those in authority the emergency communications planning envisages the pre-vention of communication among others. This would be carried out under the 'Telephone Preference System' which divides telephone subscribers into three categories:

1. those with lines 'vital to the prosecution of war and to national survival'
2. lines additional to category 1 'necessary to maintain the life of the community in a peacetime emergency'
3. all lines not covered by categories 1 and 2.

The distinction between the Categories is quite explicit according to a Home Office circular: 'Both Category 1 and Category 2 telephones are those whereby a subscriber can both receive and originate telephone calls', whereas 'Category 3 lines will only be able to receive calls.' In other words, this would mean that 95% of telephone subscribers would be cut off, and only able to receive calls, while the whole 'emergency' system HQs and their staffs would be able to communicate with each other.

Not only would communication between people be restricted in this way but information about the emergency would be strictly in the hands of the state and a Home Office circular 'Information Services in War'(7) has indicated three stages in the dissemination of such information. The first would be the transmission of information to 'allay public concern'; the second, giving practical advice; and the third, 'post attack stage' (presumably covering any full scale emergency). The main part of the media would be the War Time Broadcasting Service (WTBS) which would be manned by BBC staff and personnel from the Central Office of Information and the Scottish Information Office and which would be transmitted from a number of well-protected stations which are linked to the Regional and Zone Headquarters, each of which has its own studio facilities. In some circumstances, the Regional authority might also broadcast information of a more local nature in which case it would have ready-made facilities through the BBC (radio and TV) in Glasgow, Edinburgh and Aberdeen.

The Role of the Local Authorities

Although the reorganisation of local government in Scotland did not come into effect until May 1975 discussions between the Scottish Home and Health Department and representatives from local government on the reorganisation of emergency planning took place as early as 1972. These discussions reached agreement on a number of points including: a link at local authority level between a higher degree of preparedness for war with planning for peacetime emergencies; the nomination of a local authority chief officer as emergencies coordinator; the filling of all vacant posts of Civil Defence Planning Officers and their redesignation as Emergencies Planning Officers (EPOs). It was recommended that chief constables become responsible for co-ordinating planning although 'it would remain the responsibility of the various local authorities' chief officers to draw up plans in their own fields.'(8) As agreed, local authority planning in Scotland continued in advance of local government reorganisation itself and by 1974 every local authority had appointed an EPO. Many of these have backgrounds in the armed forces; the EPO of Lothian and Borders is Lieutenant Colonel R.G.W. Lamb, (Retd.), Strathclyde's is Air Commodore George Innes, (Retd.). Each heads an emergency planning team whose size varies with the size of the region served but includes executive officers and clerical and secretarial staff. The Strathclyde emergency planning team, for example, comprises 1 principal EPO, 3 senior EPOs, 1 senior administrative officer, 1 administrative assistant and 2 clerical officers.(9)

In addition, various officials of the local authorities have been appointed to 'designated' posts which would become operational in the event of an emergency. The chief constables of Lothian and Borders and Strathclyde are respectively the Regional Police Commanders (Designate) of the Eastern and Western Zones and various other designated posts also exist. A study of an English local authority showed that the Intelligence and Information Officer (Designate) was the public relations officer; the Communications Officer (Designate) the Director of Administration; Officer (Designate) for Billeting and Care of the Homeless the Director of housing and so on. No doubt similar appointments have been made by Scottish local authorities.

Training of members of local emergency Planning Teams and the various officials appointed to designated posts is largely undertaken by the Home Defence College at Easing-wold in Yorkshire. This was established on its present basis in 1973, and its role is defined as follows: 'The purpose of the College is to alert the higher echelons of management in local government, the armed forces and other services and in industry to what is required of them in home defence, and in particular to assist local authorities to discharge their res-ponsibilities for translating peacetime services to meet the needs of wartime and the situations posed by major peacetime emergencies.'(10) Each year thousands of officials and coun-cillors (and police officers) attend courses at the College. These courses are invariably framed within a scenario of nuclear attack or war with an external enemy but the content is applicable to a wide range of emergency situations.

The Police Role

In any emergency the role of the police would generally be to enforce such regulations as might be made by the Regional Commissioner or by any of the Controllers but they would also, according to an official manual, have 'urgent additional tasks' including the taking of 'Special measures to maintain internal security, with particular reference to the detention or restric-tion of movement of subversive or potentially subversive people.'(11) They would also be responsible for the guarding of key points and the maintenance of protected areas.'(12) In all this we would see the full implications of the various dev-elopments traced in earlier parts of this book. The work of the Special Branch (and other intelligence gathering sections of the police) would be put to use in identifying those regarded as 'subversive or potentially subversive' and therefore re-quiring surveillance or detention. It is likely that the police would be armed, the current extensive training being put to good use. Numerically, the regular police would be augmented by the Special Constabulary, which is primarily intended for use in an emergency and whose numbers would doubtless swell as they have done on the occasion of previous emerg-encies.

Special Patrol Groups (SPGs) of which there are at least two in Scotland (see Chapter 3) would perform the function of a 'third force', operating somewhere between the army and the regular police, and would themselves be supplemented by special Police Support Units (PSUs). Such units described as 'mobile contingency units'(13) would comprise about one fifth of the regular male police strength of each force. PSUs, consisting each of 35 men plus a civilian driver would be formed on a divisional basis on the instructions of the chief constable acting on a message from the Scottish Office. No special training would be given to designated PSU personnel although the Police Manual does envisage that chief constables will have opportunities to practice the units in peacetime 'when suitable policing tasks arrive.'(14) Grampian Police is the only Scottish force to have given details in recent years of PSU training; in 1980 training was given to 10 inspectors, 13 sergeants and 157 constables.

As far as present planning is concerned the Regional and Zone Police Commanders have already been designated. As stated earlier (see page 101) the Regional Commander would be the Chief Inspector of Constabulary (presently Edward Frizzell, formerly chief constable of Central Scotland Police); the Northern Zone Police Commander Designate is the chief constable of Fife; the Western Zone Commander Designate is the chief constable of Strathclyde; and the Eastern Zone Commander Designate is the chief constable of Lothian and Borders.

In addition, war duties have for a long time been part of a constable's routine training and further training is provided in more specialised aspects such as air reconnaissance. At a more senior level, officers regularly attend courses both at the Home Defence College and at a local level. In 1978, for example, 58 inspectors attended Zone Police War Duties courses, while 10 chief inspectors and 1 inspector attended a standard Home Defence course, and 13 superintendents and 5 chief inspectors attended a Police Home Defence course at the Home Defence College. In 1976, Patrick Hamill, then an assistant chief constable in Strathclyde and now chief constable as well as Western Zone Police Commander Designate, became the first Scottish police officer to attend a course at the Royal College of Defence Studies.

At a practical level every Scottish police force organises major incident simulations to test its preparedness for emergencies. In 1977, Tayside Police held such an exercise involving also the ambulance, hospital and Water Service Department; Northern Constabulary created a Major Incident Communications Room at Lerwick; Grampian Police held various exercises for offshore emergencies involving the oil companies, emergency and rescue service and (unspecified) government agencies; (this aspect of emergency planning is dealt with in more detail below); and Strathclyde Police reconvened a Working Party on Emergency Co-ordination and organised visits to various commercial and professional bodies to advise on the police role in an emergency.

In 1978 Lothian and Borders Police went somewhat further and held a joint exercise with the army and RAF in which Special Air Service (SAS) troops armed with automatic weapons flew into the old Edinburgh Airport (now only used for air freight) in what was described as an 'Entebbe-style' raid while another RAF aircraft equiped with night search stroboscopic lights circled the airport. Only a brief statement on the exercise was issued by Lothian and Borders Police to the effect that 'An exercise to test certain aspects of the major incident contingency plan of the Lothian and Borders Police is now being held. The exercise will not interfere with the normal operations of the airport and inconvenience caused to the public will be minimal.'(15)

The Military Role

If in an emergency the police were unable to perform the functions expected of them the government would call in the military—as it did in Northern Ireland in 1969—although there is no precedent for this in Britain in recent times. (The use of the army has been in a quite different role, that of strike breaking.) As noted earlier, the Home Defence Regions correspond to the Army's United Kingdom Land Forces (UKLF) districts, the headquarters of which is at Wilton near Salisbury. Scotland is one such district and is itself divided into two areas—Highlands and Lowlands divided by a line running from the

Mull of Kintyre to Fife Ness. HQ Highlands is in Perth and HQ Lowlands and Scotland in Edinburgh.

If the military were called in during an emergency a Joint Services HQ would be set up in each region under a Regional Military Commander. Similarly, there would be a Zone Military Commander to co-ordinate the services at Zone level and military units would be used with the approval of the Regional Commissioner or Zone Commissioner in response to requests from the chief constable or the relevant Controller. As has happened during war time and in Northern Ireland, legislation would be speedily passed suspending rights to bail and trial, authorising internment and restricting freedom of movement. In addition, there are, of course, many other laws, statutory and common, which would prove useful in dealing with opposition, especially those dealing with Incitement to Disaffection, sedition and so on.

A detailed description of how the military might operate if an emergency reached this stage can be had from the military's own Army Manual: Land Operations Vol. III (counter revolutionary operations), 1969. This defines as enemies of internal security 'subversives' who take 'action to undermine the military, economic and psychological morale or political strength of a nation and the loyalty of its subjects'—a wide definition not substantially different from that of Merlyn Rees noted above (see page 59). Essential to dealing with such people would be 'the forming of effective, integrated and nationwide intelligence organisation without which military operations can never be successful.' Nor can this be established suddenly, a fact of which the British state with its existing surveillance methods and intelligence gathering is well aware. According to the army's plan the 'fundamental' concept is 'the working of the triumvirate, civil, military and police as a joint and integrated organisation from the highest to the lowest level of policy making, planning and administration.... It is of paramount importance that the command of military forces remains in a military channel.' The system envisaged would be headed by a National Defence Council (which would include the military but would give the appearance of being under civilian control), under which the Regional

Government system would operate as outlined earlier in this section. Parallel to this would be the National Operations Committee which would be headed by the military but would also include the police, the Special Branch and M15, the Security Service. Similar committees would operate at Regional, Zone and probably Area level.

At a British level an important role would be played by the 8th Field Force of the army (of 10 such forces) which is committed to a Home Defence role. This would be backed up by static units in all other UKLF districts and would keep the population under control and guard key areas and sites. 'The creation of the 8th Field Force has given a cohesion and direction to the troops allocated to the Home Defence role which was lacking previously. It would appear to strengthen the Army's internal security capability in a war-like emergency, and is in line with other internal security measures adopted by the government in recent years.'(16)

2. Contingencies

The scenario with which we have so far been dealing is that of a full scale emergency when the government of the country has passed to the Regional Government System. Obviously there are a number of situations which are more limited and do not reach the stage of a full emergency. Equally obvious should be the fact that emergency planning generally can be applied to such contingencies or emergencies which are either limited to one part of the country or to a particular section of the population. The firemen's strike in the winter of 1977/78 and the lorry drivers' strike of 1979 were two recent examples of such contingencies. Both cases illustrated clearly the extent to which planning has now evolved.

As we have seen a National Security Committee (NSC) was established by the Tory government in 1972 and that this had the task of redrawing the national War Plan on the assumption of an internal enemy. But the NSC had also another job—that of planning for contingencies, that is, everything short of an emergency. This involved defining those situations in which the military could be used 'in aid of the civil power', without the declaration of a 'state of emergency' (under the Emergency Powers Act 1920) and without reference to parliament. These situations were: where the police were unable to carry out the functions expected of them, for example, in certain public order situations—Military Aid to the Civil Power (MACP); in the event of a major natural disaster, for example flooding—Military Aid to the Civil Community (MACC); and, in the event of a strike, to maintain 'essential services'—Military Aid to the Civil Ministries (MACM).

The law relating to the use of troops is complicated and far from certain.(17) In general, there are two acts of parliament which authorise the use of troops. The first and main one is the Emergency Powers Act 1920, passed in response to a miners' strike. This requires a declaration by the government of a 'state of emergency' which must be renewed by parliament every month. Its use is therefore subject to a degree of control. The 1920 act was used only six times in the fifty years to 1970, but has been used five times since then.

The Emergency Powers Act 1964 is devoid of even this limited control on the executive in that it allows the Defence Council, which is composed of five government ministers, five senior military personnel and three senior civil servants, to authorise the use of troops without any declaration of a state of emergency and without any reference to parliament to do urgent work of national importance. Until 1978 a further restraint was contained in the Queen's Regulations for the Army which stipulated that the emergency also be limited and local. It was this power which was used to bring in the army into Glasgow during the firemen's strike in 1973 and again in 1975 for the dustcart drivers strike. Both clearly were limited and local. The next occasion, however, when the 1964 act was used was that of the national firemen's strike of 1977/78 which, obviously, was neither 'limited' nor 'local' and the use of troops under the 1964 act was therefore in contravention of Queen's Regulations. The disclosure of the fact(18) led to the Defence Council's deleting from the Regulations the words 'limited and local' and so establishing far reaching powers without any reference to parliament.

Despite this change it is generally accepted that there are important practical restraints on the use of the army in industrial disputes. The first is that to do so almost inevitably exacerbates the feelings of those on strike and leads to increased conflict and a hardening of resolve. The second is the inability of the armed forces to replace civilian, and often highly skilled, labour. This has been obvious in the case of the firemen's disputes where armed forces personnel not only were clearly not up to the standard of those they were replacing but they had also to be led to the scenes of fires by the police. In the transport drivers' strike of early 1979, therefore,

the government decided against using troops and the Home
Secretary, Merlyn Rees, told parliament that the army would
be able to move only five per cent of the normal road supplies.(19)

But this same dispute, and the national firemen's strike of
1977/78 illustrated just how far national contingency planning
had advanced. In what the Minister of Transport, William
Rodgers, described as 'a unique occasion with no precedents'
the Cabinet approved the setting up of 11 Regional Emergency
Committees to monitor the strike, liaise with the unions
involved over supplies, and prepare for the use of troops and
police. These committees, activated by the Cabinet Office
Civil Contingencies Unit (CCU) which had replaced the
National Security Committee in November 1974, were based
on the Department of Transport's Traffic Areas and co-
ordination at a national level was dealt with by a team of
officials based in the Department of the Environment's
Emergency Operations Rooms. This team reported every four
hours to 10 Downing Street.(20)

At a Scottish level the Scottish Central Co-ordinating Committee believed to have comprised 30 or so representatives
from the various sections of the Scottish Office, the Departments of Trade, Industry, Energy and Employment, the police
and the army, was serviced by two duty rooms at the Scottish
Economic Planning Department in Glasgow and in Old St.
Andrews House in Edinburgh.(21) Special emergency committees have also been set up at regional level. Thus for example
during the firemen's dispute Strathclyde Regional Council set
up a Fire Emergency Committee composed of the chief
executive, the Director of Administration (within whose department the Emergency Planning Team functions), the Fire-
master, the Deputy Chief Constable, a representative from the
Department of Public Relations and half a dozen councillors
most of whom were also members of the Police and Fire Committee. Similarly a Special Committee on Emergencies was set
up during the oil tanker drivers' dispute and was reconstituted
during the haulage drivers' dispute. Invariably, when these
committees have met the public has been excluded and only
the barest details have appeared in the Regional Council
Minutes.

3. North Sea Oil

The development of North Sea Oil since 1968 has posed a number of problems for policing. At one level, there has been the question of the policing of offshore installations in terms of crime detection and prevention: at another the threat, supposed or real, to these installations from an 'enemy', external or internal.

The Continental Shelf Act 1964 extended the jurisdiction of British criminal and civil law and the powers of the police to cover sea based installations within British Designated Waters, and made it clear that, from a policing standpoint, all incidents occurring on offshore installations are regarded as if they occurred onshore. In addition, by 1967 the Home Office had evolved what is known as the 'port of operation' formula which decides which police force is responsible for policing particular installations. According to the formula, offshore operators nominate a 'port of operation' for their installations and the police force covering this port then has responsibility for the installations as well. In effect, this means that the oil and related companies choose the force under whose jurisdiction they will operate. In practice, nearly all operators in the North Sea have nominated Aberdeen as their 'port of operation' since the first rig began drilling in 1968. Policing the North Sea installations is therefore largely the responsibility of Grampian Police. The work involves about 50 rigs and other installations and a daily average of 8,000 workers, and Grampian Police have specially trained teams of officers for investigations offshore. Close co-operation has also been established with the Norwegian Police at Stavanger as a result of problems caused by those oil fields close to, or cutting across, the international line between the U.K. and Norway. Problems of jurisdiction have also occurred in relation to barges operating in North Sea Oil and one incident in particular, which occurred in 1976, has been cited by Grampian's chief constable in support of an argument for reform of the law. The incident in question related to alleged fire-raising on a barge which was registered in Panama, owned by a Dutch Company and chartered to an American company. The police attended as requested by the oil company but it became clear that they were acting beyond their powers since the vessel was Panamanian registered and also operating in international wasters. Chief Constable Morrison argues that the police had a moral obligation to attend and that: 'It does not appear logical that, while this barge was operating within 500 metres of the platform, it was subject to British Criminal Law by virtue of Section 3 of the Continental Shelf Act, 1964, but yet doing exactly the same work outside the 500 metre zone was subject to Panamanian Law....It would seem reasonable, therefore, that some measures should be taken to amend the Continental Shelf Act, 1964, to deal with these contingencies.'(22)

Of greater concern to the state and the oil companies is the supposed vulnerability of oil installations to terrorists and military enemies, and emergency planning involving the police, armed forces, private companies and government departments has developed considerably, especially since the mid 1970s when there was a proliferation of conferences, seminars and working groups on the question of such threats. These groups included not only representatives of the interests already mentioned but also included a number of prominent academics from Scottish universities including Professor John Ericson from Edinburgh and David Greenwood from Aberdeen. The potential threats to North Sea Oil have been seen from a number of sources. A conference sponsored by the Atlantic Treaty Association at the Royal Naval College, Greenwich in 1975 'attended by high ranking NATO navy and air officers, civil servants, oil men, MPs and academics'(23) saw the main danger from Russia trying to obtain political leverage by the harassment of oil installations in a time of tension.'(24) Others have seen the main threat in the shape of terrorists who could either sabotage or destroy installations, or hold them and personnel on them to ransom. Whatever terms they are framed in, these discussions and the ensuing actions have much wider implications. Occasionally these are spelled out. Thus, for example, at the 'Offshore Europe 75' conference in Aberdeen in 1975, Professor D.C. Watt of the London School of Economics called for the creation of a special force of marines to protect installations, claiming that the ability to shut off oil supplies was 'a very significant instrument of political pressure, **whether for striking trade unionists or for politically motivated terrorists.'**(25)

In fact, four years later it was announced by the Ministry of Defence that a special commando unit of 300 Royal Marines was to be set up to guard the Clyde submarine base and to protect the various North Sea installations. To be known as the Commachio Company, the unit is to have its own high speed vessels, helicopter back up, and will be on permanent stand-by.(26)

In the article on the policing of the North Sea already cited Chief Constable Morrison is rather reticent about preparations for emergencies saying 'Apart from giving an assurance that all appropriate action is being taken, I do not think it is in anyone's interests to spell out existing arrangements for dealing with this type of contingency.' However, it is known that, in general, security precautions on oil rigs are the responsibility of the operators but there is clearly close liason between them, the police, the Armed Services and the Department of Energy.(27) In addition, a trade paper, 'The Oilman', reported in 1978 that in addition to police-military planning, the oil companies involved in the North Sea were drawing up plans with MI5, the Security Service.(28) Such planning almost certainly involves screening of potential employees and in any case at least one major operator in the North Sea, Shell, has admitted its use of the Economic League's 'service' of vetting job applicants for previous trade union activity. Shell's personnel director has said of the League: 'They give us pretty good value....We are interested in identifying overt opponents of the system to which we are committed. The last thing we want to do is to have political subversives on our payroll or on sites in which we have an interest.'(29) Shell are unlikely to be alone in their interest and their concept of 'political subversives' is sufficiently vague to cover anyone who has shown an interest in the basic rights of employees. In addition, Irish workers on the rigs and other installations are periodically subjected to detention and questioning under the Prevention of Terrorism Act mainly at ports of entry.

In preparation for possible emergencies, exercises involving all three armed services are held two or three times each year under the codenames 'Purple Oyster' or 'Prawn Salad'. These sea-going exercises generally involve Royal Marines from the headquarters of 45 Commando Group in Arbroath being flown out to the installation in question by Sea King helicopter. In the event of an emergency the military would act under the general direction of the local chief constable (although firing orders would remain with the military commander) and once any threat was eliminated the situation would revert to the police. In addition, gas and oil installations are regularly patrolled by the Royal Navy using three or four island class vessels built after the mid '70s alarms. Although emphasis was originally placed on their role in fishery protection the Ministry of Defence now describes them as 'the first step in an integrated patrol network round gas and oil installations.... they will also carry out fishery protection duties'.(30)

Emergency planning in relation to North Sea oil may appear more justifiable and less open to the kind of criticism (made at the beginning of this section) which may be made of other forms of such planning. However, the one has to be seen as an integral part of the other and in any case it should be obvious that a number of problems are posed for civil liberties—in the relationship of the police to the military, in the vetting and screening of potential employees, even in the jurisdiction applicable to offshore installations. (In 1977, for example, workers involved in an industrial dispute on a production platform claimed that they had been told by management that they were in mutiny and that the Royal Navy would be called to remove them from the rig.) The recent erosion of civil liberties in Britain is often justified by reference to 'emergencies' of one kind or another and such erosion has invariably outlasted the 'emergency' which gave rise to it. Emergency provisions of whatever kind demand more scrutiny, not less.

NOTES

1. See especially Bunyan.
2. For the story of these disclosures see
   The RSGs, by Nicholas Walter (Solidarity 1963), Inside Story, No. 8 March/April 1973, and Laurie.
   The RSG for Scotland was situated at Barnton Quarry on Corstorphine Hill, west of Edinburgh. It was maintained at least until the mid-1970s when four youths were prosecuted for theft of radio equipment from the site, described in court as 'office premises'. See Daily Telegraph, 30.6.74. Undercurrents, May/June 1975.
3. State Research Bulletin No. 8.
4. The Guardian, 12.6.75.

5. Laurie, pp. 254-7.
6. Time Out, 21.3.80.
7. ES2/1975 (Home Office circulars are not circulated to Scotland but are generally replicated by Scottish Office circulars).
8. Municipal Yearbook, 1973, pp. 128-9.
9. Strathclyde Regional Council Minutes, 7.12.77. p. 1165.
10. Municipal Yearbook 1977, p. 69.
11. Police Manual of Home Defence, p. 26.
12. ibid.
13. ibid p. 20.
14. ibid p. 24.
15. The Scotsman, 15.4.78.
16. State Research Bulletin No. 8.
17. See 'The Law and the Use of Troops in Industrial Disputes' by Christopher Whelan, Working Paper No. 2, Centre for Socio-Legal Studies, Wolfson Hall, Oxford, and the background paper 'The Use of Troops and Police in Strikes' in State Research Bulletin No. 4.
18. State Research Bulletin No. 4.
19. The Guardian, 19.1.79.
20. Time Out, 18.1.79.
21. City Lynx (Edinburgh), 1.2.79.
22. 'North Sea Oil: the role of the Police' by Alexander Morrison, Police Studies, Vol. 2, No. 1, Spring 1979.
23. Daily Telegraph, 20.6.75.
24. Daily Telegraph, 30.6.75.
25. Financial Times, 20.9.75., emphasis added.
26. Glasgow Herald, 31.8.79.
27. Hansard. 26.6.78.
28. 13.5.78.
29. The Guardian, 9.6.78., quoted in State Research Bulletin No. 7.
30. The Scotsman, 19.7.78.

CONCLUSION

In this short study I hope to have raised a number of important questions, even if I have attempted few answers. I have tried to show that policing was not neutral in the past as official histories and accounts would have us believe (even though it has performed necessary social functions) and that the existence of a police force continues to present a number of problems from a civil liberties point of view, problems of which we are only just becoming aware and which we are very far from solving.

The key question is that of accountability. It applies as much to day to day methods of policing, for example to intelligence gathering and the use of Special Patrol Goups, as to more controversial and overtly political aspects such as the work of the Special Branch; it determines how those who are policed and who pay for the police through rates and taxes can exert some measure of control on a public service. This book, hopefully, has shown that such control is all but absent and that this should give cause for concern. There is clearly, then, a need to ask such questions as where such accountability should lie and how it can best be achieved, and to encourage public and informed debate on such issues. If there is no such debate and soon, then it will quickly become all the more difficult to influence the pattern of policing or to exert any meaningful control.

This is not to suggest that policing should become a tool of any particular political faction. (Opponents of greater police accountability have insisted that this is an inevitable result. Given their own influence and the increasingly political stances of the police this is somewhat disingenuous). It is to say that policing in a democratic society must be responsive to the real needs and wishes of that society and that these needs and the possible solutions can only be identified by informed and open discussion which involves equally all those concerned.

Such informed discussion and public accountability must apply also to the kind of 'emergency planning' described in Part Three although, undoubtedly, questions will continue to go unanswered 'in the interests of national security' or because they are not 'in the public interest'. But the 'public interest', if it is to have any meaning, must of necessity involve the public or else be exposed for the cynical sham it is.

At a time of increasing authoritarianism, expressed in the law, policing, policy statements, attitudes and the manufacture of news opinion through the media, the question of who guards the guards takes on a greater significance and importance than perhaps ever before. If all that this book has done is to pose that question, to provide some information as a basis for its discussion and to stimulate further enquiry, then it will have been worthwhile.

APPENDIX

The Criminal Process in Scotland

The criminal process in Scotland (and much of the criminal law) is fundamentally different from that in the rest of the United Kingdom and while a complete study of criminal procedure is beyond the scope of this pamphlet a basic understanding of the most important features is essential to an understanding of the police in Scotland.(1)

Procedure

Procedure in Scottish criminal courts is either summary or solemn. Under summary procedure the case is heard by a judge sitting alone with no jury, when the charge against the accused is set out in a document called a complaint. Under solemn procedure the case is heard by a judge sitting with a jury and the charge is set out in an indictment. An accused in Scotland has no right to opt for trial by jury and the mode of trial is either determined by statute or by the prosecution. (This is dealt with below.) Juries in Scotland are composed of 15 persons (and not 12 as is the case in England and Wales) and there are three possible verdicts—guilty, not guilty and not proven. A verdict of not proven has the same effect as a verdict of not guilty, that is the accused is released and cannot be tried again on the same charge. All verdicts are (and traditionally have been) by simple majority, eight votes of guilty being sufficient to convict. It has been suggested that the number of 15 jurors emerged in the sixteenth century as the mean of the three most frequently found numbers of jurors—13, 15 and 17—and therefore the most frequently resorted to.(2) The same author also suggests that it is not the Scottish practice on jury verdicts which requires explanation but rather the English requirement of unanimity which is strange. Defenders of the Scottish against the English system usually point to the Scots system of public prosecution and the requirement in virtually all cases of corroborative evidence as offering additional safeguards against wrongful or doubtful conviction.

The Courts

The superior criminal court in Scotland is the High Court of Justiciary which is based in Edinburgh but which sits on circuit in other cities and major towns as necessary. Procedure is always solemn and trials are normally heard by one judge sitting with a jury. Only the High Court can deal with cases of murder, rape, treason and incest (and a few others). Subject to statutory provisions the High Court has unlimited powers of imprisonment and fine.

The bulk of Scottish criminal business is dealt with in the sheriff court which can sit under either solemn or summary procedure. Scotland is divided into a number of sheriffdoms (which are sub-divided into sheriff court districts) headed by a sheriff-principal, assisted by several sheriffs. Appointment as sheriff is made by the Lord Advocate from either the advocate (barrister) or solicitor branches of the legal profession. A sheriff sitting with a jury may impose imprisonment for up to two years. Sitting summarily he may impose no more than three months imprisonment (although six is occasionally competent) and a maximum fine of £1,000.

The lowest criminal court is the district court which is presided over by a lay magistrate, appointed by the Secretary of State for Scotland, advised on points of law by a legal assessor. Procedure in the district court is always summary and the maximum sentences which can be imposed are 60 days/ £200 fine. In Glasgow there are also three full time stipendiary magistrates who are legally qualified and have the same sentencing powers as a sheriff summary court.

Appeal against conviction or sentence from any court is heard by the High Court sitting as an appellate court, usually by three judges, although more may sit in cases of importance or complexity. There is no appeal in criminal cases to the House of Lords nor is re-trial possible.

Criminal Prosecutions

Criminal prosecutions in Scotland are essentially public, that is they are normally conducted by full time prosecutors acting in the public interest. The police in Scotland **never** prosecute. (Certain other officials for example from H.M. Customs and Excise, H.M. Factory Inspectorate, local authorities, may be authorised to prosecute for breaches of specific statutory provisions.) Prosecutions are controlled by the Lord Advocate, who is a political appointee and the principal law officer of the Crown in Scotland, assisted by the Solicitor General (also a political appointee) and by several advocates-depute, that is advocates (barristers) employed by the Crown. Known collectively as Crown Counsel they are assisted by a permanent staff of civil servants headed by the Crown Agent, based at the Crown Office in Edinburgh.

The Lord Advocate is responsible for virtually all prosecutions in Scotland although the actual conduct of such prosecutions is delegated to the advocates-depute in the High Court (and occasionally in the sheriff court) and to the procurator fiscal in the sheriff and district courts. The procurator fiscal is a full time civil servant, legally qualified, appointed by, and under the control of, the Lord Advocate. A procurator fiscal (colloquially known as the PF or fiscal) is supported by a number of appointed deputes and assistants for each sheriff court district.

Private Prosecution

While, as noted above, some officials may prosecute in what is basically a quasi-public capacity, few other individuals besides the public prosecutors may initiate or conduct criminal prosecutions in Scotland. Landowners have a specific statutory authority to prosecute poachers and such prosecutions are not uncommon but this is probably the only major exception to the public nature of prosecution in Scotland.(3) The victim of an offence or a person agrieved has no power to prosecute nor, generally speaking, to influence the prosecutor's decision to prosecute.

This has resulted from a gradual process beginning in 1587 when the King's advocate was given the power to prosecute 'although the parties be silent or would otherwise privily agree' and was therefore entitled to prosecute without the concurrence of a private party, or to pursue a prosecution which had previously been abandoned. This developed into the situation where no private party could prosecute without the concurrence of the Lord Advocate. The last time that a private prosecution occurred without such concurrence was in 1909 when the High Court granted leave to a party to prosecute for fraud after the Lord Advocate had declined to prosecute. More recently, in 1961, an official of a union of youth clubs sought to prosecute a seller of 'Lady Chatterley's Lover', the Lord Advocate having refused either to do so himself or to concur in a private prosecution. The official, Mr. McBain, alleged that he had 'suffered a personal and political wrong as a result of the sale of the book, both because he had been shocked and outraged by reading it, and also because of his special concern with the morals and welfare of young people.' The High Court rejected his application for a Bill of Criminal Letters (which would have allowed him to prosecute) on the grounds that the wrong complained of was a public, not a private, wrong, and as such was open to prosecution by the Lord Advocate only. Except in the instances mentioned therefore, private prosecution can be said to be non-existent in Scotland.

The absence of a right of private prosecution is double-edged. On the one hand it does mean, for example, that private prosecutions such as have been initiated in England by Mary Whitehouse against Gay News (for blasphemy) and by Francis Bennion against Peter Hain (for the Stop the Seventies tour), could not have occurred in Scotland. (This is not however to presume that such prosecutions could not have occurred at all. They could in theory have been initiated by the public prosecutor).

On the other hand it means that individuals are deprived of what is at least a theoretical remedy for injustice. Probably the most illustrative recent case of this kind was that of Paddy Meehan. Meehan had been convicted of murder in 1969 and sentenced to life imprisonment. As part of his unceasing attempt to establish his innocence he sought in 1974 (and again in 1975) to initiate a private prosecution against three police officers for perjury at his trial, following the refusal of the Lord Advocate to do so. His application by way of applying for a Bill of Criminal Letters was heard by three High Court judges and was turned down on the grounds that allowing the application 'would open the floodgates to private prosecution which our system of criminal prosecution has been devised to prevent....' Meehan, who was eventually granted a Royal Pardon in 1976, wrote later of this: 'The major problem: a Bill of Letters can only be issued by the courts: in other words you had to get the court's permission to go to court.(4)

The Role of the Police

The role of the police in relation to the criminal process in Scotland is therefore considerably more restricted than that of the police in the rest of the U.K., being limited essentially to the investigating and reporting of offences to the public pro-secutor. They neither initiate nor conduct prosecutions and when police officers appear in court they do so only as wit-nesses. Their role is 'where an offence has been committed... to take all such lawful measures, and make such reports to the appropriate prosecutor, as may be necessary for the purpose of bringing the offender with all due speed to justice.'(5)

In theory, the police have little discretion in deciding whether to report someone for an alleged offence and they are generally expected to do so when there is sufficient evidence to justify the taking of proceedings. In cases of doubt as to the sufficiency of evidence the decision is supposed to be that of the procurator fiscal, not of the police. In practice, as is the case in all systems of policing, a great deal of discretion is exercised 'on the streets' in cases of minor infringements of the law, with the police merely warning, informally, alleged offenders. This is particularly true in relation to 'street of-fences' such as obstruction and breach of the peace, where the definition of the offence is so wide as to permit the exercise of extensive discretion.

The investigation of crime is ultimately the responsibility of the procurator fiscal, not of the police, and the police are bound to follow his instructions. The Police (Scotland) Act 1967 states that: '...in relation to the investigation of offences the chief constable shall comply with such lawful instructions as he may receive from the appropriate prosecutor.'(6) In minor cases, to be dealt with in the summary courts; the investigation is normally left to the police themselves, but in more serious cases, the procurator fiscal may attend at the scene of a crime, will frequently order the police to make further and specific enquiries, and will, after receiving the police reports, interview witnesses for the prosecution himself.

The Decision to Prosecute

After receiving the initial police report the procurator fiscal must decide whether to prosecute. (Even though the police may and frequently do charge suspects the ultimate decision about whether to proceed is for the procurator fiscal and not for the police. The police charge may therefore be confirmed, dropped or a different charge substituted.) In certain cases, he must report to the Crown Office for instructions but generally the decision is his and before proceeding he must normally be satisfied that the facts ascertained constitute an offence and also that, in terms of the rules regarding admissibility of evidence and corroboration, there is sufficient evidence to justify proceeding. It is not for the procurator fiscal, however, to make a judgement as to the credibility of the evidence. In addition, the fiscal may decide to exercise his discretion to order 'no further proceedings' if the offence is of insufficient importance or if the accused has sufficient excuse for his/her actions.

If the fiscal decides to proceed he must first of all decide on the charge—in many cases he will simply confirm the charge initially made by the police. He must then decide on the mode of trial, that is whether to proceed under summary or solemn procedure. In some cases, the mode will be stipulated by statute, as it is in the cases of murder, treason, rape, etc. which must be tried in the High Court, and in the case of some minor offences which can only be tried summarily, but otherwise the fiscal has considerable discretion and in making his decision will generally consider the gravity of the alleged offence, and whether the accused has any previous convictions. In 1978, over 224,000 cases were taken on complaint and less than 4,000, less than 2%, on indictment. If he decides on solemn procedure, the fiscal will interview possible prosecution witnesses, making his own note of the interview, and will send this together with any other evidence to Crown Counsel. Crown Counsel may instruct further enquiries, may order that no further proceedings be taken, that the charge be dealt with under summary procedure in the sheriff court, or solemn procedure in the sheriff court or in the High Court, and such instructions are binding.

While in occasional cases the Lord Advocate may instruct a fiscal to proceed with a prosecution where he has previously declined, there is in general no way in which the Lord Advocate can be compelled to prosecute. Although he is a government minister and answerable to parliament for the way in which he conducts his office, he is under no obligation to discuss his reasons for prosecuting or not doing so.

Police Questioning

The Judges Rules and Administrative Directions to the Police which govern (or are supposed to govern) police questioning and interrogation in England and Wales do not apply in Scotland where the police operate under rules laid down in cases by the courts and, to a lesser extent, in statute. The rules are complex and open to various interpretations and discussions of them, for the sake of convenience, generally divide police enquiries into three stages:

1. before the police have reasonable cause to suspect any particular person of having committed the offence;
2. where a particular person may be suspected but not yet charged; and
3. after charge.

In the first stage, it is clear that the police may question anyone without administering a caution but that no one has any obligation to answer. (Many statutes make it obligatory in certain circumstances to provide one's name and address when required by the police to do so and, in addition, the Official Secrets Act and the Prevention of Terrorism (Temporary Provisions) Act 1976 both make it an offence to fail to provide information.) Any statements made by a person at this stage are admissible as evidence in court.

At the second stage, the position becomes complex. One important view was that laid down in 1954 in the case of Chalmers(7), a case which was decided by a full bench of the High Court. This included opinions to the effect that: 'There comes a time however, when a police officer, carrying out his duty honestly and conscientiously, ought to be in a position to appreciate that the man whom he is in process of questioning is under serious consideration as the perpetrator of the crime. Once that stage of suspicion is reached, the suspect is in the position that thereafter the only evidence admissible against him is his own voluntary statement.'(8), and 'The theory of our law is that at the stage of initial investigation the police may question anyone with a view to acquiring information which may lead to the detection of the criminal; but that, when the stage has been reached at which suspicion, or more than suspicion, has in their view centred upon some person as the likely perpetrator of the crime, further interrogation of that person becomes very dangerous, and, if carried too far, e.g. to the point of extracting a confession by what amounts to cross-examination, the evidence of that confession will almost certainly be excluded.'(9) These, then, were quite strict rules and, emanating as they did from a full bench of the High Court, of considerable authority. Their effect over the ensuing two and a half decades however has been considerably diluted by a progression of other cases. For example, in the case of Thomson(10), Lord Wheatley told the jury: '… if the police in the course of a very difficult and serious investigation have got to keep asking questions and probing and probing and probing, then as long as they are doing that fairly having regard to their task and their duty, and that nothing infavourable or unfair to the accused was done either by word or by deed or by trickery, then, of course, anything that they can elicit is normally competent and acceptable evidence.' More recently, in the 1979 case of Hartley(11), a statement made by a 17 year old youth who had been held in police custody for over 12 hours, without sleep, who had been questioned a number of times but had not yet been charged and who finally broke down and confessed to the murder under investigation, was ruled admissible.

The rules of admissibility have therefore been progressively widened over a period of years in favour of the police. Indeed, in the case of Hartley, Lord Grieve went so far as to say that the test of fairness meant not only fairness to the accused by 'fairness to those who investigate crime on behalf of the public.'

At the third stage, after charge, no further questions by the police are permissible and only a purely voluntary and spontaneous statement by an accused will be admissible in court.

Appearing in Court

A person arrested must normally be brought before a court not later than the day after he is taken into custody, unless this is a day on which the court is not sitting. In serious cases, to be tried on indictment, the accused is brought before the sheriff in private and may be released on bail (unless charged with murder or treason) or committed for further enquiry for a period of no more than eight days after which he must be fully committed 'until liberated in due course of law'. (Full Committal). As a safeguard a person detained in custody before trial must have his trial concluded before the period of custody from full committal exceeds 110 days. The '110 day rule' is strictly adhered to and will only be suspended where delay is clearly not the fault of the prosecution, for example where the accused has been ill and unable to be brought to trial. The rule was suspended generally in March 1979 when court officials who were members of the Civil and Public Servants Association took industrial action in support of a pay claim.

The '110 day rule' applies only to cases to be dealt with

under solemn procedure and there is no similar provision in summary cases.

To a large extent therefore, the Scottish police lack the direct involvement in the criminal prosecution system of their colleagues in England and Wales. This has not prevented the police organisations from taking part in the debate about the criminal process although, as I have argued elsewhere (see chapter 8) it has contributed to the absence of chief constables of Scottish forces from the ranks of the new public and expressly political police chiefs. In terms of practical policing however, other than the practice of police officers normally patrolling in pairs in order to satisfy the Scots law requirement of corroborative evidence in nearly all cases, there appear to be few differences which result from the different legal systems.

NOTES

1. The standard textbook on criminal procedure is Renton & Brown. The SCCL's 'Your Rights' is the best practical guide for the lay reader.
2. Willock, pp. 189-90.
3. Game (Scotland) Act 1832.
4. Meehan, p. 173. See also Kennedy.
5. Police (Scotland) Act 1967 s.17.
6. ibid.
7. Chalmers v H.M. Advocate (1954 JC 66).
8. ibid, Lord Justice-Clerk at pages 81-2.
9. ibid, Lord Justice-General at pages 78-9.
10. Thomson v H.M. Advocate (1968 JC 61).
11. Hartley v H.M. Advocate (1979 SLT 26).

BIBLIOGRAPHY

Ackroyd, C., Margolis, K., Rosenhead, J., Shallice, T.: *The Technology of Political Control* (Penguin, Harmondsworth, 1977)

Adam, H.L.: *The Police Encyclopedia* (Vol. 1) (Blackfriars, London 1910)

Bunyan, T.: *The Political Police in Britain* (Julian Friedmann, London 1976)

Chief Constables (Scotland) Association—*Centenary Brochure* (Chief Constables (Sc) Association, Glasgow 1969)

Encyclopedia of the Laws of Scotland (Green, Edinburgh, 1930)

Flood, M., Grove-White, R.: *Nuclear Prospects* (FOE/CPRE/NCCL, London 1976)

Glasgow 1919 (Molendinar Press, Glasgow 1975)

Grant, D.: *The Thin Blue Line; the story of the City of Glasgow Police* (John Long, London 1973)

Hain, P. (ed.): *Policing the Police* (volume 2) (John Calder, London 1980)

Hart, J.: *The British Police* (Allen & Unwin, London 1951)

Hattan, W.: *Complaints Against the Police* (Mimeo, Glasgow 1974)

Hewitt, P.: *Privacy; the information gatherers* (NCCL, London 1977)

Irvine, H.: *The Diced Cap; the story of Aberdeen City Police* (Aberdeen City Police, Aberdeen 1972)

Johnston, T.: *History of the Working Classes in Scotland* (Unity, Glasgow 1946)

Hobsbawm, E.J.: *Industry and Empire* (Penguin, Harmondsworth 1973)

Kennedy, L.: *A Presumption of Innocence* (Panther, St. Albans 1977)

Kibblewhite, L., Rigby, A.: *Aberdeen in the General Strike* (Aberdeen People's Press, Aberdeen 1977)

Laurie, P.: *Beneath the City Streets* (Granada, London 1979)

Logue, K.: *Popular Disturbances in Scotland 1780-1815* (John Donald Edinburgh 1979)

MacShane, H.: *No Mean Fighter* (Pluto Press, London 1978)

Mark, Sir. R.: *Policing a Perplexed Society* (Allen & Unwin, London 1977)

Marshall, G.: *Police and Government* (Methuen, London 1965)

Mathieson, W.: *Church and Reform in Scotland* (Maclehose, Glasgow 1916)

Meehan, P.: *Innocent Villain* (Pan, London 1978)

Mill, J.: *The Scottish Police - Powers and Duties* (Green, Edinburgh 1944)

Milne, Sir. D.: *The Scottish Office* (Allen & Unwin, London 1957)

Police and Constabulary Almanac (Hazell, St. Albans, 1979)

Prebble, J.: *The Highland Clearances* (Penguin, Harmondsworth 1969)

Quinault, R., Stevenson, J.: *Popular Protest and Public Order* (Allen & Unwin, London 1974)

Rait, Sir. R. & Pryde G.S.: *Scotland* (Benn, London 1954)

Reith, C.: *A New Study of Police History* (Oliver & Boyd, Edinburgh 1956)

Renton, R.M., Brown, H.H.: *Criminal Procedure* (Green, Edinburgh 1972)

Rule, J.: *Private Lives and Public Surveillance* (Allen & Unwin, London 1973)

Scotland's Regions 1978-79 (Culross, Coupar Angus, 1978)

Scottish Council for Civil Liberties: *Your Rights: a guide to civil liberties in Scotland* (Polygon, Edinburgh 1980)

Scottish Police Federation: *Golden Jubilee Brochure* (Scottish Police Federation, Glasgow 1969)

Seth, R.: *The Specials* (Gollancz, London 1961)

Sheehan, A.V.: *Criminal Procedure in Scotland and France* (HMSO, Edinburgh 1973)

Sillitoe, Sir. P.: *Cloak Without Dagger* (Cassells, London 1955)

Smout, T.C.: *A History of the Scottish People 1560-1830* (Collins, Glasgow 1972)

Stair Society: *Introduction to Scottish Legal History* (Stair Society, Edinburgh 1958)

Walker, D.M.: *Scottish Legal System* (Green, Edinburgh 1976)

Webb, K.: *The Growth of Nationalism in Scotland* (Molendinar, Glasgow 1977)

Wilcox, A.F.: *The Decision to Prosecute* (Butterworth, London 1970)
Willock, I.D.: *The Jury in Scotland* (Stair Society, Edinburgh 1966)

ARTICLES

Anon: *Interrogation and the Test of Fairness* (Scots Law Times 6.7.79)

Gordon, G.H.: *The Institution of Criminal Proceedings in Scotland* (1968 Northern Ireland Legal Quarterly 249)

MacLean, Iain: *Red Clydeside, 1915-19* (in Quinault & Stevenson)

Mitchell, J.D.B.: *The Constitutional Position of the Police in Scotland* (1962 Juridical Review)

Richards, E.: *Patterns of Highland Discontent, 1790-1860* (in Quinault & Stevenson)

OFFICIAL REPORTS AND PUBLICATIONS

Annual Reports of Her Majesty's Chief Inspector of Constabulary for Scotland 1969-78

Annual Reports of the Chief Constables

Report of the Tribunal appointed to inquire into the allegation of assault on John Waters (Cmnd 718) HMSO 1959

Royal Commission on the Police—Final Report (Cmnd 1728) HMSO 1962

Handling of Complaints Against the Police (Cmnd 5583) HMSO 1974

Criminal Procedure in Scotland (Second Report) (Cmnd 6218) HMSO 1975

Computers and Privacy (Cmnd 6353) HMSO 1975

Computers: Safeguards for Privacy (Cmnd 6354) HMSO 1975

Report of the Committee on Data Protection (Cmnd 7341) HMSO 1978

The Interception of Communications in Great Britain (Cmnd 7873) HMSO 1980

PRINCIPAL STATUTES

1724   Disarming Act

1833   Royal Burghs (Scotland) Act (3 & 4 Will.4 c46)

1839   County Police Act (2 & 3 Vict. c65)

1847   Burgh Police etc. (Scotland) Act (10 & 11 Vict. c39)

1850   Police (Scotland) Act (13 & 14 Vict. c33)

1857   County Police Act (20 Vict. c2)

1862   General Police and Improvement (Scotland) Act (25 & 26 Vict. c101)

1889   Local Government (Scotland) Act (52 & 53 Vict. c50)

1892   Burgh Police (Scotland) Act (55 & 56 Vict. c55)

1919   Police Act

1967   Police (Scotland) Act

SCOTTISH COUNCIL FOR CIVIL LIBERTIES

The Scottish Council for Civil Liberties is an independent voluntary organisation which exists to protect the rights and freedoms of individuals and groups in Scotland. It is affiliated to the National Council for Civil Liberties but decides its own policy and is responsible for its own finances.

SCCL CAMPAIGNS for changes in the law by briefing and lobbying Members of Parliament and by submitting evidence and arguments to official committees on law reforms. It ADVISES people of their rights, taking up individual cases and referring others for specialist assistance. It EDUCATES through fact sheets, pamphlets and reports on civil liberty issues. In recent years SCCL has worked in the areas of criminal justice, police procedures and police accountability, prisons, mental health, education, public order, censorship, the rights of young people, and the provision of legal services.

SCCL is a membership organisation. Membership is its most important source of income and is open to all who accept the aims of the Council. Organisations and groups may affiliate. To defend civil liberties and your rights SCCL needs your membership.

Current membership rates are:

Couples	£6.50 (£6 by bankers order)	
Individuals	£5	(£4.50 by bankers order)
Non wage earners	£2	

Membership forms are available on request—or simply send your name and address with the appropriate fee to SCCL, 146 Holland Street, Glasgow G2 4NG.